Praise for
Even in Our Darkness

It doesn't happen often, but every once in a while, a gripping book comes along that is profoundly unmasked, unsettling, and unforgettable. I couldn't put this down: This is one devastating, thought-provoking, and needful read that will change the landscape of your soul.

> ANN VOSKAMP, *New York Times* bestselling author of *The Broken Way* and *One Thousand Gifts*

Even in Our Darkness is filled with the raw pain, beauty, mystery, and grace that our hearts were meant for. There are no religious platitudes or ethereal ideas in these pages, just God's grace and affection washing over a family time and time again through the highs and lowest of lows. I found the vulnerability and transparency of this book to be shocking, and a desire arose in me to live all the more in the light as God is in the light. This book will encourage you, and I pray it will warm your heart toward the affections that Christ has for you.

> MATT CHANDLER, lead teaching pastor of The Village Church and president of Acts 29 Network

We all have our times of darkness when our circumstances are difficult, with no idea of where God's presence is. It is one of the most painful human experiences possible. Jack Deere speaks on a vulnerable, raw, and honest level about his own narrative and the darkness he has encountered, both around him and within his own soul. He ultimately points the reader to the God who is always there and who always sustains.

> DR. JOHN TOWNSEND, *New York Times* bestselling author

I've known Jack Deere for nearly forty-five years. Or at least I thought I knew him. After reading his memoir, I became truly acquainted with my longtime friend for the first time. I cried. I gasped for air. I laughed. And I worshiped God. For Jack's story is really a story about friendship with a God whose love and faithfulness are constant, whether we are on top of the mountain or walking through the valley of the shadow.

SAM STORMS, pastor of Bridgeway Church in Oklahoma City and past president of the Evangelical Theological Society

How do we make sense of the pain and evil in this world, and who is this good God who has allowed it? This powerful and poignant book goes a long way toward answering that for all of us. Written beautifully and harrowingly—and so grippingly that you won't want to stop reading—this story is everyone's story. If a few of us could be nearly as transparent and honest as Jack Deere is here, the light of Christ would shine far brighter in our culture, turning many hungry hearts toward himself.

ERIC METAXAS, #1 *New York Times* bestselling author of *Miracles*, *If You Can Keep It*, and *Martin Luther*

Many pastors write memoirs, but no pastors write memoirs like this. Jack Deere takes us into a world of "evangelical nobility" that is as pocked and flawed as any we Christians like to pretend we are above—and then plunges us into the torrents of a family disintegrating in the Class 5 rapids of a tragedy. Raw, gritty, and transparent, Jack's writing rings with effervescent joy and searing pain. I read the last seventy-five pages with my heart in my throat and tears in my eyes. Even before I finished, I was making a list of friends to whom I plan to send this book. If I could, I'd send every person reading this a copy myself. It's that good.

LYNN VINCENT, #1 *New York Times* bestselling author of *Same Kind of Different as Me* and *Heaven is for Real*

Dr. Jack Deere's brilliantly written memoir of his extraordinary life is a must-read for any person who has come from a dysfunctional family. Jack shows the wonderful possibility of peace passing understanding when traumatic circumstances would dictate otherwise.

> R. T. KENDALL, author of more than fifty books and former minister of Westminster Chapel

We fell in love with Jack Deere's son Scott, never dreaming it would forge a friendship with Jack and Leesa. Jack's raw and gritty exposé of his life demonstrates beauty in imperfection and love that is refined through hardship.

> NANCY DUARTE, CEO and author

This is a gut-level story that leaves no illusion that life can be defined by man's religion. I've known Jack Deere and his family for more than thirty years. I've watched and walked with him during some of the events covered. The story is real. God's love always shines through the darkness.

> DUDLEY HALL, author and president of Kerygma Ventures

I feel privileged to have witnessed this book being lived before it was written, as my mentor Jack Deere showed by example how to savor God's friendship through our darkest days. This story inspires hope, not by sanitizing reality, but by artfully displaying a transcendent reality—the beauty of God even in our darkness.

> MICHAEL ROWNTREE, senior pastor of Wellspring Church, North Richland Hills, Texas

Even in
Our Darkness

Even in
Our Darkness

A Story *of* Beauty *in a* Broken Life

JACK DEERE

ZONDERVAN®

ZONDERVAN

Even in Our Darkness
Copyright © 2018 by Jack S. Deere

This title is also available as a Zondervan ebook.

This title is also available as a Zondervan audiobook.

ISBN 978-0-310-53817-2 (International Trade Paper Edition)

Requests for information should be addressed to:
Zondervan, *3900 Sparks Dr. SE, Grand Rapids, Michigan 49546*

Library of Congress Cataloging-in-Publication Data

Names: Deere, Jack, author.
Title: Even in our darkness : a story of beauty in a broken life / Jack Deere.
Description: Grand Rapids, MI : Zondervan, [2018]
Identifiers: LCCN 2017050239 | ISBN 9780310538141 (hardcover)
Subjects: LCSH: Deere, Jack. | Christian biography. | Christian life.
Classification: LCC BR1725.D377 A3 2018 | DDC 277.308/3092 [B]—dc23 LC
    record available at https://lccn.loc.gov/2017050239

Cover design: Brian Bobel
Cover photo: iStockphoto.com
Interior design: Kait Lamphere

Printed in the United States of America

18 19 20 21 22 23 24 25 26 27 28 /DCI/ 15 14 13 12 11 10 9 8 7 6 5 4 3 2

For Scott—

thanks for the laughter,
thanks for the tears,
and thanks for the prayers beneath heaven's altar.
Good-bye for now, Scotty boy,
but only for now.
Love,
Dad

One

On the morning of December 31, 2000, I watched a white cardboard coffin travel up a conveyor belt into the belly of a Boeing 757, along with the other baggage. The body in that coffin had belonged to my son. But he had gambled with it once too often.

Twenty-one years earlier, I had watched him sprint into a door-jamb. The collision rocked his blond head and knocked him on his butt. I held my breath and braced for wails. Instead, he jumped up, laughed, and galloped off to his next crash.

As Scott grew, the collisions became less physical, but they still occurred regularly. When his second-grade teacher handed him a homework assignment he didn't like, he crumpled it up and tossed it over his shoulder.

He discovered drugs in our church parking lot about the same time he hit puberty. But he never allowed the dysfunction of addiction to steal his greatest gift: the ability to make people fall in love with him.

He swayed cops with a smile and was only warned when they caught him driving drunk or with pot. He would buy himself a place to stay for another six months with an offer to mow a friend's lawn. His jokes brought invitations to dinner.

Not only was he charming, but he was also lucky—usually. When his car was totaled and his buddies were carried off with broken bones, Scott waltzed away without a scratch.

Scott had some clean months, but mostly he lived from one high to the next. We lived from one crisis to the next.

After he turned twenty-one, he told me about a dream in which he had died and lay in a fetal position. It was so real that he felt his spirit leaving his body, and he looked down on his corpse. He awoke, surprised that he was still alive and that he lay in the same fetal position as in the dream.

"What do you think the dream means, Dad?" he asked. "And why did I wake up in the fetal position?"

I didn't hesitate to answer. I was familiar with warnings that come in the night to pierce the indifference of our waking hours.

"It means you will die if you don't change," I said.

"I want to change."

"I know you will, Scott."

He would get clean for a few weeks, and his mother and I would grasp for the hope that maybe it would last.

A year after that dream, he was home for Christmas. He popped his head into the TV room after dinner to tell us he was going out with his girlfriend.

It was the last time I saw him smile.

He said, "Good night, Dad."

I said, "Good-bye, Scott."

An odd story flitted through my mind. A few hours before his death, Abraham Lincoln told his bodyguard good-bye. A twinge of guilt passed through me. Why did I say "good-bye" to Scott instead of "good night"? The foreboding didn't make sense. He seemed clean for the past couple of weeks. He had enrolled in college. In the morning, his mother planned to take him to Target to buy dishes, a comforter, and cleaning supplies for his new apartment in Bozeman, a mere three hundred miles east of our home in Whitefish, Montana.

The next morning, I sat downstairs in the living room by the fire. Above the mantel, two elk hung high on the wall, my first rifle kill and my first bow kill. I was writing my next book on my notebook computer, until the noise of a malfunctioning DVD player broke my concentration. It came from Scott's room.

I walked upstairs and opened the door.

Then I turned and ran for the phone.

"Is he breathing?" the 911 operator asked.

The word *no* stuck in my throat. I couldn't say it. "No" meant I couldn't bring him back. "No" meant I had no faith. "No" was final.

But it was the truth.

"No," I said.

Then I raced upstairs to try to bring my son back from the dead.

After the paramedics put my son into a body bag and carried him out of our home, my wife and I, along with Scott's brother and sister, descended our mountain and checked into a local resort. We could not sleep in the same place where Scott lost his last bet spinning the cylinder of a revolver.

I woke up in our hotel room as the sun crept around the edges of the curtains. Out of habit, I started to pray the same prayer I had prayed every morning for years: "Father, pro—" Then I remembered. I choked on the word *protect*. I could not get it out.

I suppressed a disdainful laugh.

I wasn't ready to give up on God, but it felt like he had given up on me. I could not reconcile my theology with the nightmare we were now living. Weren't prodigal sons supposed to come home?

I thought I had insured Scott's life with the promises of God and my prayers. "Take delight in the LORD, and he will give you the desires of your heart," King David had written. Had I not delighted enough, or was I deceived about what my heart desired?

"Ask and it will be given to you," Jesus told his followers. I had asked every day for years. I hadn't just asked; I had believed as well. And according to Jesus, belief in the promises is supposed to make them work for you. Had I not believed enough? Or were the promises empty?

For decades, I had preached that the mystery of suffering would always elude our understanding. It was an easy thing to say, until the weight of that mystery crushed me. I didn't know how to get out from under it, except to flee to the place where I grew up. So with Scott's body in the luggage bay, I sat in the Delta Airlines 757, surrounded by strangers, hurtling south through the sky. Then a voice spoke into my shock and confusion. It was so faint, so ephemeral, that I might have made it up.

Hold my hand, I thought it said.

I could hardly picture that hand.

But it was there, and always had been—guiding me through the rage-drenched home of my youth, thrusting a wrench into familial patterns of purposelessness and poverty, and blow by blow, destroying the illusion that I could earn the gifts it bears.

In the beginning, everything was formless and void, but his Spirit hovered over the deep, dark, and violent waters.

Then he spoke: "Let there be light."

He saw that the light was good. Although the dark was not good, he allowed it to remain. But he separated the light from the dark. He called the light "day," and the dark "night."

And against that great vault of night, he flung stars to serve as guideposts and as a reminder that light was always pushing through the darkness.

I am old now, and my night is near. But his first commandment still resounds, gaining strength as it conquers space and time.

When I open myself up to his light, the end feels more like a beginning, a flicker at dawn that spreads until everything radiates under the noonday sun.

And all I can see is his beauty.

Two

I am the descendant of drinkers and drifters better at passing on their love for the bottle than family history, so I have been left with few details about the soil from which I grew.

Dad never spoke of his father, but he did take his name—"Jack." His mother had named him Jewel because he was her jewel, but that name was too feminine for him.

He was born in Sabine, Texas, but was raised on a Mississippi farm during the Great Depression. Just before the start of the Second World War, he enlisted in the Navy. He transferred off a battleship a few months before the Japanese blew it up at Pearl Harbor. Dad escaped injury for the rest of the war, except for a shrapnel wound that left him with a huge knot of scar tissue in the middle of his back. The bomb exploded on the deck of his new battleship, and Chief Petty Officer Deere carried men into the sick bay for two days before a sailor told him his back was bleeding.

On leave in 1942, he visited Handley, Texas, a rural community east of Fort Worth, where howling coon dogs guarded the night and crowing roosters ushered in the morning.

Dad first laid eyes on Mom at the soda fountain in the drugstore. She was sixteen. He was twenty-one. Wanda Jean Barley also hated her first name and only answered to Jean. They married shortly thereafter.

When he was discharged after the war, he went to work at the General Motors assembly plant in Arlington, and they moved into a two-room shack behind my maternal grandparents' house. I was born two years later in the vanguard of the baby boomers.

Dad stood only five foot eight, but he had the broad shoulders of a taller man. He parted his black hair on the left side. His eyes were brown, and his complexion was dark. To me he looked like Glen Ford, the movie star of the fifties.

My first memory is Dad carrying me through the basement of the Leonard Brothers department store in downtown Fort Worth. His strong arms never put me down to rest. He smelled of the Brylcreem that made his hair shiny, Aqua Velva shaving lotion, and cigarettes. I pointed at a display of pocketknives by the cash register and begged for one that looked like the knife he carried. He bought me a huge knife, but it was rubber. When he handed it to me, I complained.

I was two-and-a-half years old.

Although he was raised in an environment that produced hard workers, not critical thinkers, Dad was both. He knew the answer to every question I ever asked him.

"How far away is the moon?"

"Approximately 240,000 miles."

"What about the sun?"

"Ninety-three million."

"How hot does the water need to be before it boils?"

"Two hundred twelve degrees."

Dad taught me all these things and more before I was ever forced to sweat through a Texas September afternoon in a cramped desk.

I worshiped Dad for more than his intelligence. In the war, he taught hand-to-hand combat. He showed me how to throw a punch, how to block one, and how to take a man to the ground—valuable skills for a poor boy growing up in 1950s Texas.

"Did you kill anyone during the war?" I asked him.

"Yes," he said.

A vacant look passed over his face, and though I pressed, he wouldn't offer any more details. I was glad he killed the enemy. It made him seem tougher.

He was the first person to tell me about God and sin. God is all-powerful, all-knowing, and ever-present, he said. God created the world out of nothing, and the devil, a fallen angel named Lucifer, introduced evil into our world by tempting Adam and Eve to sin.

In my own life, it didn't take long for the prohibition of sin to provoke sin.

It never occurred to me to put gravel in the gas tank of our 1950 Chevy until Dad said, "Jackie, never put gravel in the gas tank of the car." The harder I tried not to think about it, the more obsessed I became, until I scooped up a fistful of pea gravel from our driveway and shoved it in the tank. I paid for the pleasure of that sin with a whipping from Dad's belt.

Dad told me we were born with immortal souls. After we died, our soul would be happy in heaven forever or tormented in hell by endless fire.

But beyond saying grace before meals and reciting bedtime prayers, we did not talk to God in our family. While I believed in God's existence, I did not believe in God. I believed in Dad, who did fine supplying our daily bread.

Mom dropped out of high school in the eleventh grade to marry Dad. I never saw her read a book. She offered me tenderness in the place of knowledge.

She called me "honey" as often as she called me Jackie.

At naps and bedtimes, she dragged her long nails across my back, moving only her hand and not her fingers, whispering to me all the while. The heel of her palm barely touched the smooth, tan skin of my back. I wanted those back scratches to last forever. Sometimes they did, and I fell asleep.

I was proud of Mom because she was pretty. She was five foot four, with flawless, fair skin. Her waist was small, but she was not skinny. She passed her brown hair and blue eyes down to me.

Every morning, Dad hugged and kissed Mom before work. She met him at the front door when he came home, and they kissed again.

"There is not a man walking on the face of the earth that I would let hurt your mother," he once told me. "I would put him down."

By the time I turned six years old, my two brothers, Gary and Tommy, had joined us. We had moved out of the shack behind my grandparents' house and into a two-bedroom rental house on Yeager Street, a gravel road north of the bowling alley.

My brothers and I sprinted through our earliest years in the stability of a simple time and place. Houses were small, and yards were large. Leaves weren't blown; they were raked and burned. The smell of burnt leaves signaled that fall was here, not the smell of firewood, for no one had a fireplace in our neighborhood. All our houses were drab on the inside, but no one knew that, for no one had ever heard of interior decorators. Fast food and TV did not yet rule our evenings. Mom cooked our supper, and we all ate it together at the kitchen table. Every night, Dad presided over supper. He thanked the Lord for our food and then taught us how to eat the meal in courteous peace without sound effects—no clicking our teeth against the fork, no smacking our lips, no chewing food with our mouths open, and no slurping our iced tea.

My favorite picture of this happy childhood was taken on the morning of my sixth Christmas. I stood in the front yard of our rental house on Yeager Street, Tommy on my left and Gary on my right; the three of us were outfitted in our new Davy Crockett suits with coonskin caps and Jungle Jim rifles slung over our shoulders.

We smiled and squinted under a sun so bright that we could not see the clouds gathered on the horizon.

Three

In 1955, the most powerful corporation in the world promoted Dad to maintenance supervisor at the General Motors assembly plant, allowing us to purchase our first house: a 992-square foot, three-bedroom bungalow that even had a hall.

Dad bought two new Chevy Coupes a few years later, and he won a writing contest, which brought us a new refrigerator and lawn mower and other prizes.

But with the prosperity, he vanished from our lives. He worked the second shift from 3:00 p.m. until 11:00 p.m., and we were asleep when he came home. Our bedtime prayers to God ceased. If Dad and Mom still kissed after work, I never saw it.

No repairman ever came to our house. Dad could fix anything. But Dad's fixing skills worked against us just like his GM job did. He did electrical, plumbing, and air-conditioning jobs before he went to work at the GM plant, and he also took on these jobs during the weekends. On those few Sundays when he was home, he napped in the living room on the one nice piece of furniture we owned—our red couch embroidered with gold thread.

Mom did everything for us. She took me to buy my baseball glove, bat, and ball. She went to all my Little League baseball games. Mom stood on the sidelines and yelled, "Let Jackie pitch." When the coach ignored her, she marched up to our bench and told him how hard I could throw. He moved me to the pitcher's mound. When I walked four batters in a row, he glared at my mom. She glared back.

She developed migraines and called our elderly family doctor to the house at night to shoot her up with Demerol. The doctor sat beside Mom's bed until she passed out.

The pain of her isolation surfaced in other ways, like when I fired my brand-new, four-shot Buck Rogers dart pistol at the TV. The darts hit the center of the TV. Their suction cups held them in place. I pulled the darts off the TV, sat back down, reloaded, and fired again.

"Jackie, stop that right now!" she said.

She went back to her ironing. I still had one dart left in the gun. I aimed my gun at the center of the TV and squeezed off the last shot.

"I told you to stop that!" she exploded.

She snatched the dart gun from my hand, threw it on the floor, and stomped it into little pieces—an angry dance to the dissonant symphony that played throughout my childhood.

I don't know what it was about the third grade that emboldened my friends and me, but the dam holding back all the damns broke. We were gloriously awash in torrents of expletives that none of us could define.

I had my back to her in the kitchen as she baked cookies when I let the f-word casually slip out.[1] For a moment, the word hung there in the air with the scent of chocolate chip cookies. Then from behind me, I heard her hand pat along the kitchen counter, grasping for a suitable weapon. She clinched a metal flyswatter and flew at me. The only part of me she did not hit was the part protected by the back of the chair in which I sat. When I tried to flee, she blocked me and intensified the beating.

My little brothers rushed in when they heard the screams.

"Why is Jackie getting spanked?" Gary asked.

1. See the acknowledgments (page 281) for why a minimal amount of coarse language in used in the stories in this book.

"I said f—k," I told them.

She exploded again. This time I dove under the kitchen table and refused to come out, until she stormed out of the kitchen.

That summer, a torrential rain pounded one afternoon. Mom left us alone to go to the store. My brothers and I stripped to our underwear and charged outside. We dove headfirst into a six-inch gulley in our backyard, treating it like a Slip 'N Slide and competing for who could glide the farthest. Mom returned home amid the celebration and shouted for us to come to the back porch. We were covered in mud and grass. She made us take our underwear off, and then she sprayed the mud off us with the spray nozzle on the garden hose. The spray stung our naked bodies. Then she marched us into the kitchen and beat us with a handful of switches, swinging, grimacing, and yelling until she had drained out all of her rage.

Every year, our home transformed more into the battleground of a war with unknowable rules of engagement. Mom gave us sweetness, laughter, and love, until one of us—usually me—stepped on a landmine buried in the wilderness of her heart.

When Dad was home, he was rarely angry; he was tired. The only memory I have of Dad's smile comes by way of a photo taken of him in his naval uniform just before he married Mom.

In the late fall of 1955, Mom went into the hospital for a complete hysterectomy. The surgeon sliced open Mom's abdomen only to find a baby growing in her womb. He sewed her back up.

At the hospital the next day, a nurse came in to change Mom's bandages. I gaped at the long, raw, bloody incision. Her stitches ran the length of her abdomen like a huge zipper. I wondered how anyone could survive a wound like that. When the nurse left, Dad took Mom's left hand in his right hand and rested their clasped hands over her womb. He knelt beside her bed, reaching out to me with his left hand. I knelt beside Dad.

"Thank you, God, for saving the life of my wife. Now please, God, save the life of my child," he prayed.

Until that moment, I had only heard recited prayers, words that you threw at a faraway God. Dad's plea summoned an immense power into the room. My skin tingled with a presence that could dissolve me on the floor or dispatch me to the stars.

The residue of that experience still clung to me when we left the hospital. At home, I asked Dad what I had to do to get into heaven. He told me that when I died, I would arrive at the gates of heaven and stand before Saint Peter. He would take out two books and a set of scales. The first book contained my good deeds, the other my bad ones. Saint Peter would place the good deeds on one side of the scale and the bad deeds on the other side.

"If the good deeds go down, you go up," he said. "If the bad deeds go down, so do you."

My heart sank.

Four

The birth of Deborah Deere on May 1, 1956, provided a brief détente between my parents and lured Dad back into the home. He stopped taking jobs on the weekends, and in the mornings before I left for school, he held Debbie high in the air and talked gibberish to her. Dad showed me how to change her cloth diaper and avoid sticking her with the pins. Dad loved Debbie so much that hope rose within me that he might become a regular presence in our home again.

But the newness of a newborn wore off, and the man I worshiped disappeared again and abandoned us to the fury born in the heart of an unloved woman.

Mom's capacity for faultfinding flourished with renewed intensity. Cops were lazy and sneaky. Church people were hypocrites. Preachers were the worst. Over and over, she told a story about the pastor who performed the funeral for her grandmother. He hung around the house, loaded up on free food for the entire afternoon, and stayed for dinner after the other guests had enough sense to let the family be alone. And then, just before he said good-bye, he uttered a statement that revealed his obliviousness to their grief.

"Well," he said, "this has been the best day."

She did not withhold criticism from her children, whose willful disobedience and innocent mistakes she repeated to others, prefaced with disdain: "You won't believe what my idiot son did the other day."

To weather that humiliation, my heart turned hard. I believe it would have completely ossified had it not been for Nonnie, my maternal grandmother.

Mom did not need to work, but the boredom of domesticity and an absentee husband drove her to a job selling burial insurance and sent us to the shelter of Nonnie.

In the summer, Nonnie made picnic lunches and took us fishing. She showed me how to bait the hook with worms and minnows. She let me stay in the kitchen while she cooked and showed me how to roll out the dough and shape it into a pie crust, how to peel carrots and dice an onion, how to cut a potato into French fries and fry them in Crisco and garlic salt.

And as soon as I could see over the steering wheel of her yellow 1961 Ford Fairlane, she taught me how to drive. She sat beside me as I whiplashed her neck letting out the clutch, and she patted my knee, assuring me I was good driver.

I was eleven years old.

She praised everything I did. And during my parents' downward spiral, Nonnie's constant affirmation was a spring of grace that allowed me to feel special against all the contrary evidence of my home.

But Mom despised her. She never passed up an opportunity to remind me that Nonnie had doted on her brother, who was thirteen years younger. Mom said that when she was a little girl, Nonnie made her brush her hair, and when Mom did not do it right, Nonnie beat her with the hairbrush. She was embittered most over being abandoned as a small child. When I asked Nonnie why she sent Mom to live with her grandparents for a few years, she said, "Honey, it was the Great Depression, and we had no food. Sending your mother to her grandmother was the only way we could feed her." Nonnie never said a bad word about Mom.

More than anything, I wanted to be like Dad, but Mom's traits rubbed off, making me critical and entitled.

The scarcity of the Great Depression produced an extravagance in the next generation who wanted to give Christmas back to their children. So every year, the one thing we could count on was being lavished with gifts.

I spent the fall of 1958 studying catalogs of model planes and engines. As Christmas approached, I picked out a huge balsa wood biplane kit and the most powerful engine to go with it. Every other day, I showed my parents pictures to avoid any mistakes.

When the day arrived, I crept into the living room while it was still dark. The lights from the tree illuminated four piles so large that you couldn't tell where one child's treasure ended and another's began.

Atop my mound was a sturdy, vinyl blue and yellow model airplane with a small engine. I recognized the indestructible trainer model for beginners from the catalogs.

How nice, I thought. *They got me two model airplanes—this trainer, which I don't need, and my biplane too.*

When they let us go at the gifts, I shoved the plastic plane aside and unwrapped box after box. Then I searched my brothers' piles, perplexed at how any parent could have made a mistake of this magnitude. Panic set in.

"Anybody see a biplane?" I asked.

Ah, I thought, *they've played a joke, like when I asked for a bicycle and it wasn't under the tree but Dad wheeled it into the living room just as my tears welled.*

Be patient, I told myself.

But denial gave way to anger as my parents picked up the wrapping paper and said, "Let's eat breakfast."

"Is that all the presents?" I asked, holding up that piece of blue and yellow plastic junk.

"Yes. Did you like yours?" Dad asked.

"This?" I said. "This is not what I asked for. I wanted the biplane with the big engine."

"I know, Jackie, but you have to learn to fly first. You would have just crashed the biplane and ended up with nothing. It's for expert fliers."

"I could have flown that biplane."

"I'll help you learn to fly this plane first, and you can have the biplane later."

"Well, you would think that the one thing a kid wanted for Christmas, he could have had."

"Go to your room," he said. "Don't come out until you can say thank you." I missed breakfast and would have missed the feast that Mom made for lunch had my father not coaxed an apology from me.

That afternoon, he helped me fly the vinyl plane. I crashed it after every takeoff.

Still, I refused to thank him, even though hours earlier I was surrounded by his gifts, unable to feel anything but anger at what wasn't there—an object of desire that I would have destroyed.

Five

One Friday night when I was eleven, Mom made popcorn. We were supposed to stay up late, watch a John Wayne movie, and then welcome Dad home from work. But a slugfest between my brothers infuriated Mom, and she sent us to bed.

"I didn't do anything wrong," I said. "Why can't I watch the movie?"

"Don't argue, Jackie. Get in bed."

She had gone too far, and so for the first time, I stood up to her.

"You are nothing but a damn shittin' rat," I said.

She sabotaged my newfound courage with one sentence.

"When your father gets home, I will tell him what you said to me."

I ran to my room, hid in bed, and tried to fall asleep, but all I could hear was: "There is not a man walking on the face of the earth that I would allow to hurt your mother. I would put him down."

I woke up that Saturday morning and looked forward to playing all day, until I remembered what I had done. This might be my last breakfast.

Dad sat at the table eating cornflakes and drinking coffee.

"Good morning, Jackie."

"Good morning, Daddy."

His expression lacked any hint of anger. She hadn't told him. I'd never felt more relieved. I looked up at her, wanting to say thank you. Mom stared back at me, her lips tight.

Later that afternoon, my brothers and I played in the huge back-yard at Nonnie's house, when Dad called me from the back porch.

"Yes, Dad."

"Jackie, come inside and go to the back bedroom."

THE BACK BEDROOM!

That damn shittin' rat! She told him!

In my grandmother's kitchen, I looked down the hall to the bedroom where my father waited. I noticed every detail on the path to my execution—the checkered, pale green linoleum floor of the kitchen, the wood planks in the hall, the little antique stand on which the rotary phone sat.

He stood at the bed. I waited for the order to bend over. But Dad had a few questions first.

"Jackie, did you get mad at your mother last night?"

"Yes sir."

"Did you call her any names?"

A lie would only make him hurt me worse.

"Uh, yes sir. I did."

"What did you call her?"

"A damn shittin' rat."

I braced for the blows, but he asked me more questions.

"Do you know what those words mean?"

"No sir. Well, I know what *rat* means."

"Would you like to know what they mean?"

"Yes sir."

"*Damn* is what people say when they want someone to be sent to hell or hurt in some other way. *Shit* is what people say when they mean *do-do*. The grown-up word is *excrement*. Or they will say they have to go shit instead of they have to go to the bathroom. Are you using any other words that you don't know the meaning of and would like to know?"

"Yes sir."

I told him my entire lexicon of profanity.

After he had defined each word, he told me people cuss because they lack the intelligence to express themselves. He said they want to appear tough, but they're not.

"Son, you are smart and strong. You don't need these words."

Then he asked, "Do you think any of those words describe your mother?"

"No, Dad, I don't. I'm sorry."

"Don't ever apply those words to your mother again."

"I won't, Dad."

I prepared to prostrate myself for the punishment. Instead Dad said, "Okay, Jackie, go back outside and play."

With Saint Peter's scales, my father painted an image of judgment that caused me to give up on God, but his demonstration of God's grace would reverberate throughout the rest of my life.

I never uttered another curse word in reference to my mother, to her face or behind her back.

Six

In 1960, Dad was promoted into the executive structure of General Motors. He wore suits to work and worked "nine to five" hours. We were on our way to becoming a wealthy family. He wanted Mom to quit work, but she wouldn't do it. Dad was home more than ever, but less available to us than ever.

I checked out a book of jokes from my elementary school library. I thought I would cheer Dad up. I told him the joke about the king who was about to hang his jester because the jester would not stop punning. At the last minute, the king had mercy on the jester and told him he would let him go free if he never uttered another pun.

"No noose is good noose," the jester said.

The king promptly hung him.

"Please stop, Jackie. These jokes aren't funny. I've heard them all," he said.

The year he became an executive, we went to church for the first time on a non-Easter Sunday. I can only guess at what brought us there: an invitation from a neighbor, the disintegration of my parents' marriage, my father's deteriorating mental state.

Sunlight poured into the sanctuary through stained-glass windows. The choir on stage wore white robes with red collars that matched the carpet, and their voices bounced off cavernous white walls.

I fidgeted in the wooden pew during much of the sermon,

which I forgot except for the preacher's story at the end about a young boy who drowned after skipping church for the swimming hole. The story was meant to evoke fear, but all I could feel was a warm, calming presence beckoning me to the front, where the preacher had invited anyone who wasn't saved.

I stood up to walk down the aisle, but Mom stuck out her leg to block my path.

"You don't need to go down there."

"But, Mom, I want to."

"You're not going down there."

I shuffled back to my seat, and the presence lifted.

There was one repercussion from our visit to the Baptist church. Two men came to our home uninvited and unannounced the next Thursday night. The men talked to Dad in the living room. Mom did not participate in the conversation. She washed dishes in the kitchen. Two things stood out to me about that visit. My father had a Bible and could discuss its contents with these professional churchmen. Several times the men said, "That's right, Jack." The second thing was that my father made a passionate statement about believing in Jesus Christ. The men also agreed with Dad. I had no idea who Jesus Christ was.

The men never visited us again, and we never went back to church.

Not long after that Sunday, Mom asked Dad to move the refrigerator so she could paint the kitchen, but he lost track of time, and as he left for work, she yelled at him.

"I'll do it when I get back," he said.

"You never do anything I ask you. I have to do everything around this damn house," she screamed.

Then she flew at him, slapping and scratching. He absorbed some blows, but he did not hit back. He held her wrists, dodged her kicks, and pleaded with her, "Jean, please stop it. Please. I'll take care of it."

I could not understand how a man who had killed the enemy in the war had become afraid of the woman he had vowed to protect. It frightened me to see Dad afraid of Mom.

In the rare moments I had with Dad when Mom was not around, there were inklings of a shift toward darkness.

At a bowling match with some of the men from work, a friend poured whiskey into Dad's Coke.

"Don't tell your mother about this, Jackie," he warned.

"Don't worry," I said, happy to share the secret.

Later, I was alone with him in the kitchen when I overhead a phone conversation with Nonnie.

"After New Year's, I'm getting out," he said.

On January 21, 1961, Dad woke to an empty house, poured whiskey in his coffee, swallowed some barbiturates, and scribbled an angry note.

Sometime before noon, he walked over to the record player in front of the two windows in our living room. He put on Floyd Cramer's "Last Date," setting the turntable to repeat. Then he sat down on the red sofa with gold embroidery and picked up his childhood rifle. He shoved one .22-caliber shell into the chamber, pressed the muzzle between his eyes, and left a thirty-four-year-old widow with a tenth-grade education to care for his four children.

Mom came home from a half day at work that Saturday afternoon. She must have had some guess of what lay on the other side of the front door because she paused when she heard the song stop and restart. She left and returned with her father, the man we knew as Poppa.

She waited in the front yard while Poppa entered the house. When he came back out, all he told her was, "Jean, don't go in."

She fainted on the sidewalk.

We had spent the day at Nonnie's and went to sleep not

knowing what had happened. On Sunday morning, Nonnie sat on the edge of my bed and shook me awake.

"Jackie, your father is dead."

"How did he die? A car wreck?"

"No, honey. He shot himself."

I buried my face in the pillow and pretended to cry. I never told anyone about those fake tears.

An hour before the funeral, Mom held my hand as we stood beside Dad's casket. He wore one of his new suits, dark blue with a red tie, and looked like he might wake up any minute. I searched his forehead for the outline of the bullet hole, but the morticians had done their job. I obsessed over that bullet. It was the smallest made and weighed less than a tenth of an ounce. How could something so tiny inflict so much damage?

His funeral was held in the funeral home. We had neither church nor church friends to comfort us. I don't remember a single word that was said at his funeral or who said it. I did not cry.

What I do remember is the scene at the grave. I had seen funerals in cowboy movies. The bereaved wife threw the first handful of dirt on the coffin. Mom did not do that. She threw herself on Dad's coffin and wailed as the gravediggers tried to lower it into the ground. Poppa had to pry Mom off Dad's casket.

———

It wasn't until six weeks later that I began to grasp the irreversible nature of his last act. I woke up one bright Saturday morning and walked down the hall to my parents' bedroom. I wanted to ask Dad a question. As I touched the doorknob, I remembered that Dad was not there and never would be there. I felt a stab of pain. The smartest man in the world would never again answer my questions.

For weeks after the funeral, Mom dragged all four of us to the grave in the afternoons. She said she wanted to be close to Dad. We stayed until after dark, hungry and shivering in the cold.

After one cemetery visit, I watched Mom shudder as she walked through our living room. She said the living room felt cold. I went back in to feel the chill for myself, but there was no change in temperature. I stared at our red couch with the gold thread. It once held delirious joy for us on birthdays and Christmas mornings. Now I searched our couch for traces of Dad's blood. I wondered how they had managed to wipe every vestige of his last minutes off our happy couch.

I walked over to the record player and looked down at the 45 rpm single labeled "LAST DATE" in all capitals.

I found Mom at the kitchen sink. I showed her the record. Then I walked to the trash container next to the white refrigerator Dad had won in the writing contest. I looked back at Mom and broke "Last Date" into little pieces.

She didn't say a word. She smiled at me. Tears ran down her cheeks.

Even at twelve, I understood: he had turned a seven-inch piece of black vinyl into a weapon and set it to repeat so it would accuse her as she stood over his dead body.

Seven

Dad had surrendered to Mom's rage while lashing out at it, killing himself to maim her. But he had also crippled me.

In his war against her, had he considered the collateral damage? Was he also angry with me? If I had been a better son, would it have kept him alive?

These questions had no answers. But I would ask them over and over, only to hear silence in return.

We soon stopped talking about Dad and his death altogether. No one bothered to tell my little brother Tommy that Dad had killed himself. He learned about it the next school year on the playground when his classmates used the information to taunt him.

Mom must have thought that the pain would go away if we could just forget Dad. But everything in our house reminded us of Dad. I played with his tools, ran my hand over his clothes still in the closet, and picked his books off the shelves. None of us would sit on the red and gold couch.

Mom couldn't stand living there. She used most of the insurance money to buy us a nice three-bedroom brick home far away from North Hampshire Street. Our new home in east Handley on Norma Street had air conditioning and two bathrooms and carpet like the houses of the rich folks.

"Now my kids will always have a roof over their heads," Mom proclaimed.

I dreamed that I saw Dad burning in the molten caverns of hell.

I told no one about the dreams. There was no one to tell. I could not burden Mom. She had her own nightmares to fight.

I pushed away any thoughts of God and heaven, for there is no forgiveness in Saint Peter's scales.

In all that silence, a voice appeared in my head.

It told me I would kill myself before I turned forty just as Dad had done.

I also kept that a secret.

Eight

Mom took off work for a few weeks after the funeral, but then she had to go back to work. We were too young to be left alone and not the easiest flock to shepherd.

We lived on a busy corner, and my brothers and I entertained ourselves by staging a skit for the passing motorists. I stood on the roof of our house with a bow and arrow aimed at my brother Gary on the curb. Gary had strapped a piece of Styrofoam to his chest, covered it with a ketchup-smeared T-shirt, and stuck an arrow through his shirt into the Styrofoam. His back was to the traffic. As cars neared, he raised a hand pleading, "No, please, no! Don't shoot!" I let the arrow fly. It disappeared into the grass between his feet, sometimes missing his privates by six inches or so. Gary screamed and fell backward, with a bloody arrow protruding from his heart.

People slammed on their brakes. Once a woman threw a Coke over everyone in the car.

Some jumped out to help.

At that point, we ran.

The first housekeeper Mom hired left after a couple of weeks. So did the next one. And the one after that left after one day.

My mom's father had never laid a hand on me while Dad was alive, but now he took over my discipline, administering beatings at Mom's request.

At fifty-five, Poppa's cheeks already sagged into jowls. His black hair had thinned to a few strands in the middle of his head, but it still covered his back and shoulders. Sometimes he made me give him massages, forcing me to run my fingers through that sweaty mat of fur and oily skin. Nonnie claimed he was once handsome, but he was always ugly in my eyes.

His name was Ralph Barley Sr. He worked as a pressman for the *Fort Worth Star-Telegram* newspaper.

When he was drunk, he talked about his womanizing in front of Nonnie. She ignored it and didn't complain much about his gambling losses either, except to say that he would die over a poker table. But no matter how he tried, Poppa couldn't change Nonnie's fondness for me.

So he hated me all the more.

After Dad died, Mom left us at Poppa and Nonnie's house more often. In the evenings, Poppa stripped down to his undershirt and boxer shorts and sat on his throne—a red vinyl rocking chair in the corner of his bedroom. Gray padding poked through its ripped seat. The TV flashed in the other corner. He chain-smoked Raleigh cigarettes until he went to sleep. As he watched Andy Griffith and Ed Sullivan, Poppa's flatulence was as constant as the cicadas outside their window. Everything about that room stank.

Poppa had a love-hate relationship with his son, Ralph Jr. One evening, I sat on the trunk of our 1957 Chevy in our driveway and watched my twenty-year-old uncle square off against his father. Mom tried to get between them.

Poppa slipped his right hand into his back pocket and pulled out a pocketknife with a six-inch blade. He had stuck a tiny piece of paper into the slot holding the blade, causing the point of the blade to protrude from its case. Poppa opened the knife with one hand by catching the point on the seam of his back pocket.

"That's right, old man; hide behind a woman's skirts," taunted my uncle.

"Lemme go, Jean; move out of the way," said my grandfather.

His diction had dissolved into that familiar drunken slur. As he prepared to stab his son, he staggered in the summer breeze.

My uncle couldn't see the knife. Neither could Mom.

She begged her brother to leave, and then Ralph Jr. stepped back and climbed into his car.

"Aw, Jean, I could have taken care of him," said Poppa.

———————

As far as I knew, only one black person had ever crossed the threshold of our house: the maid of a friend who needed to use the bathroom. Mom cleaned the toilet with disinfectant before she allowed us to use it again. The summer after first grade, I wandered off in the Piggly Wiggly to the water fountains at the back of the produce section. The sign over one of them read "COLDER." I took a long drink.

Then I felt Mom clenching my arm, jerking me away from the fountain. She bent down until her face was a few inches from mine and lowered her voice.

"Don't drink that water," she said through clenched teeth.

"But, Mom, I want the colder water."

"Don't argue with me, damn it. That's not colder water, you dummy. It's water for the coloreds."

When Mom introduced us to Bobbie, I couldn't believe my eyes. Bobbie was black.

She worked for pennies, didn't complain about answering to irate neighbors, and knew the unwritten rules. In the mornings, she took out the cheapest plastic glass in our cabinet and set it on the counter next to the faucet. She drank out of that cup and no other.

She cooked our meals, washed and ironed our clothes, cleaned our house, and laughed at our jokes—even a few that ran contrary to her Southern Baptist sensibilities.

One Sunday, after I had smarted off, Poppa dragged me into his garage. It reeked of mildew and sheltered wasps, scorpions, and the occasional snake. With his left hand, he picked me up by my belt, dangling my seventy-five-pound frame in the air. With his right hand, he grabbed a used fan belt off the wall. I thrashed with all my might, thinking I could break his grip, but the more I thrashed, the harder he beat me. Finally, I surrendered to the lashes. He threw me onto the dirt floor and promised there was more to come.

I lay there for a second, surveying the extent of my injuries: bruises, cuts, a scraped elbow and knee.

As I dusted myself off, I made a promise of my own. When I was older, I told myself, I would beat the hell out of that flatulent pig, even if I had to creep up behind him with a club. I never got the chance.

He died a year later as Nonnie had predicted. The bet was to him. He laid his cards on the table, bowed his head, and folded for the last time.

It was the only funeral I ever attended during which I struggled to conceal my joy.

Nevertheless, Poppa's foul stench had pushed me toward a source of light.

Instead of watching TV in Poppa's bedroom, I escaped to a wooden rocking chair in the living room and read. I learned how to throw knives as I absorbed the stories of buffalo hunters and Indians. I loved Buck in Jack London's *The Call of the Wild*. I devoured the *Iliad* and the *Odyssey*, along with Roman and Norse mythology.

Ignorance. Unfaithfulness. Cruelty. I despised them all.

Thanks to him.

In the evenings, Mom came home from work and poured W. L. Weller bourbon into a highball glass of 7 Up and drank one after another. Sometimes she didn't come home until late. I heard her stumble through the garage late one evening. She made it to the kitchen, but then teetered. I caught her just before she fell, carried her to her bedroom, and put her in bed.

"My head hurts so bad."

"I'm sorry, Mom. Do you want me to call the doctor?"

"No, honey. I'll be alright."

I massaged her forehead for a few minutes. Then I walked to the wall and turned the light off. Mom groaned. I walked back to her bed and sat down on the edge. I leaned over to kiss her on the forehead. I kissed her eyelid instead. I couldn't see her in the dark.

"I love you, Mom."

"I love you, Jackie."

After I turned fourteen, my uncle, Ralph Jr., paid us a visit. We sat on bar stools at our kitchen counter. I made both of them a Weller and 7 Up. Then I made myself a whiskey sour. Mom and my uncle retreated to her bedroom.

I mixed a second whiskey sour, went into Mom's bedroom, and plopped down on the edge of her bed. They played strip poker on the bedroom floor. My uncle had Mom down to her bra and panties.

When Mom didn't come home after work, and my brothers and I had taken off for the evening, Bobbie refused to leave Debbie alone. She took her home to the 1.75 square miles of rundown apartment buildings in southeast Fort Worth, the predominant African-American community in the area. It was named Stop Six after the sixth stop on the train from Dallas to Fort Worth.

When we brothers fought, which was often, Bobbie begged us to stop. She looked like she was about to cry, and after a while, it dawned on me why. She had witnessed the beatings that resulted whenever we forced her to call Mom. She was trying to protect us. And then something else became evident: she loved us. Still, I didn't understand. Black people weren't supposed to love white people.

Different men wandered in and out of our lives. Rich men. Not-so-rich men. Tall men. Short men. Smart men. Stupid men. Married men. Single men. They all had one thing in common: they didn't stick around for long.

At the lake one Saturday, a man fondled Mom in front of us all day long.

As I mourned the loss of the woman who once cheered at my ball games, Mom met a man who was too good to be true.

His name was Jim Kenemer. He was Mom's age and divorced.

He had black hair, brown eyes, and a ruddy complexion that made me think he had Indian blood. He owned a gas station in a bad section of town and gave me a job there on the weekends. He reminded me of Dad.

And Mom treated him like she had treated Dad. When she had too much to drink one evening and attacked him, he gently held her off.

She yelled, "I'm in the driver's seat for nine months!"

"Jean, please," said Jim.

"Listen, buster, I'm in the driver's seat for the next nine months."

"Jean, your children are here. I can't believe you're saying this in front of your children."

Was Mom pregnant? Did she have an abortion? I never found out.

A year after they met, Jim helped a friend move and fell out of the back of a pickup. He slipped into a coma for eighteen hours and then died.

Mom started drinking beer in the mornings on the weekends, switching to bourbon in the afternoons.

When I was fifteen, I told Mom I was going out for the evening.

"No, you're not," she said.

"Watch me."

She slammed a highball glass full of bourbon and 7 Up against my temple, not hard enough to break the glass but enough to insult and scare. I held her arms like Dad had done.

But instead of pleading with her, I pinned her to the wall and laid down the law.

"You've hit me for the last time," I told her. "I'm bigger and stronger. From now on, I will come and go as I please, or I will just go."

She stared at me in shocked silence. I felt her arms go limp, and I let them go. She looked down at the wooden floor of my bedroom.

I turned away from her and walked out into the night.

Nine

Not all the dreams about Dad were nightmares. In some, I never wanted to wake up. These were the ones where it had all been a mix-up. Dad was still alive. We were a family again. But the morning always brought fresh reminders of a casket.

At fourteen years old, I walked past the baseball diamond in Handley Park on a Saturday morning to see my friend Tommy and his dad on the field. Tommy stood over the batter's plate. A large canvas satchel full of baseballs sat next to his father on the pitcher's mound. As he threw each ball, the father instructed his boy on hitting curve balls, fastballs, and sliders. I was in awe.

I considered myself a better athlete than Tommy and wondered what it would have been like to have the money for all those baseballs and to have someone show me the nuances of a sport.

Instead I played different games. They often involved guns.

My friend Curt, a tackle on the football team, was sprawled out on the top bunk bed in my bedroom talking to a girl on the phone. I had taken all the lead pellets out of a 12-gauge shell earlier that day, but I had left in the compressed cork wadding. My friends watched me shove the shell into my gun, thinking it was a live round.

"Get off the phone, Curt," I said smiling, "or I will blow your ass off."

Curt laughed and continued talking.

I pointed the semiautomatic 12-gauge shotgun at Curt's butt and clicked the safety off.

"Curt, I'll give you one last chance."

He didn't even look up. So I squeezed the trigger.

The room disappeared in a flash of fire and smoke. The thunder of the explosion rang in our ears. For a second, everyone thought Curt was dead. Curt thought he was dead. The wadding hit him like a sledgehammer. His body contorted and bounced a foot off the bed. He shrieked and grabbed his powder-burned, bruised butt. Then he realized he was still alive. Everyone laughed. Even Curt.

My primary group of friends consisted of seven athletes. Our parents had a lot in common. They were divorced or getting divorced; they were alcoholics or were becoming alcoholics.

One friend's father took pictures of his wife nude in different poses. His son found them, and we passed them around while we were at his house.

Mom let me use her white 1960 Cadillac Coupe DeVille for my dates. I found the perfect spot to pursue my greatest desire: a lonely hill parallel to Bridge Street that rose fifty feet above the street and overlooked downtown Fort Worth.

I picked up my girlfriend and drove the Coupe DeVille there. We turned the car off. We turned the radio on. Then we turned each other on—for two hours. I had hoped for more, but I had to get her home. When I turned the ignition, the car refused to start. *Crap.* The radio had drained the battery. I had fifteen minutes to return my date to her father. So I came up with a plan: roll the car down the hill to the main road and convince some passerby to jump-start the battery or give us a ride.

I put the shift into neutral, opened the door, and pushed against the ground with my left foot.

The big car rolled backward. Everything seemed under control. But I was about to discover a fatal defect in 1960s' automotive engineering: the power steering and brakes on a Coupe DeVille won't operate if the engine isn't running.

As the car picked up speed, I jammed my foot against the brakes. The steering wheel would not turn. We gained momentum. All we could do was hope for a soft landing and brace for the impact.

We were probably going about thirty miles an hour when we hit the telephone pole. The impact drove the back bumper into the trunk and bounced the six-way electric front seat off the tracks and smashed my left forefinger between my knee and the steering wheel.

Blood squirted from my finger onto my girlfriend's white dress. I now had fourteen minutes to get her home. But I doubted the wisdom of taking a fifteen-year-old girl home with blood on her dress.

A couple saw the wreck, stopped, picked us up, and took us home. They smirked when I said we were only talking.

My girlfriend staved off her father's wrath with a story that I'd been playing a pocketknife game with some of the guys and cut my finger. I was surprised he believed her.

By the end of the summer, it was clear to the four of us that our girlfriends would not surrender their inhibitions. So we looked south toward the Rio Grande for an initiation. I told Mom I was going to Mexico to a whorehouse with three of my friends.

"You are not going to do that, Jackie," she said.

"I am," I said, grinning.

"No you're not."

In our confrontation in my bedroom, I had broken something in her, and she gave up trying to control me. Her softening had drawn us closer, and now our relationship resembled a friendship.

Later that afternoon, I left a note hanging over the kitchen stove. The note said I would be in South Texas and Mexico for the next few days and not to worry. I signed it:

Arriba,

Jackie

We piled into my friend Philip's 1960 four-door, white Chevy Corvair and pulled out of my driveway shouting, "Arriba, Arriba!" Philip rammed the gas pedal to the floor, and we bounced south all night long on Highway 81 at a hundred miles an hour in the Corvair—the car that had inspired Ralph Nader to write the book *Unsafe at Any Speed.*

We spent the weekend at our friend Kenny's home in south Texas near Laredo. His parents were divorced. He spent summers with his dad in south Texas and the school year with his mom in Fort Worth.

That weekend, we got some girls throwing-up drunk. The girls' parents were so angry that Kenny's father kicked us out.

We parked the Corvair on the Texas side of the border and walked across the Rio Grande into Nuevo Laredo. We found a bar with private rooms in the back. Some of the girls looked as young as fourteen. Mine was a woman, maybe thirty. I was the last to go. I had spent most of my money on barbeque and beer and had five dollars left. The prostitute's price was ten. I didn't disagree. I just held out my empty hands. She ended the negotiation with a sigh.

"Come with me."

The act was awkward from start to finish. Afterward, I thought, *Is that all there is to it?*

It was the first time for all of us. We drove all night back to Fort Worth, congratulating one another, telling aggrandizing stories of what we did in that back room.

We were men now.

We all fell asleep except Philip, who kept the accelerator of the Corvair jammed to the floorboard.

It was still dark when I slid out of the Corvair and went into my house. I tiptoed to my bedroom. What I'd done didn't seem funny anymore. I didn't want to talk about it. As the sun rose, fear gripped me—a dread from another world I knew nothing about. I felt like I had broken a fundamental law of the universe, and one day I would have to pay for my crime.

———————

At the end of the summer, eight of us stood in a wooded field eighty yards apart.

The game was our version of "Last Man Standing."

We aimed 12-gauge shotguns high to create an arc for the lead pellets. The goal was to sting the guy with a few pellets, not to break his skin, though sometimes you did break the skin. A "sting" meant you were out. You knew you had hit the guy because no one could keep from yelling, "Ow!"

The contest ended with me and Les, the starting halfback, standing twenty yards apart, pointing our 12-gauge shotguns at each other, safeties off, fingers on the trigger.

Both of us shouted for the other to surrender.

Ten

The summer before our sophomore year, Bruce chased a blonde named Dixie to a church camp, but instead of catching the girl, he caught religion. It was the worst kind: Southern Baptist hellfire-and-damnation religion.

Of all my friends, Bruce was the most intelligent—and the most anxious. In the sixth grade, Bruce wore Nixon buttons to school and told anyone who would listen to vote for Nixon. He used words like *apogee* and *fistula* in daily conversation, had headaches often, and drank Dr. Pepper in the morning to get going. For his jump shot, he held the ball at his chest and shoved it toward the basket instead of flipping it with his wrist.

Despite his neurotic nature—or maybe because of it—girls felt safe with him. They talked to him for hours on the phone and told him about their secret crushes, their parents' problems, and even about their changing bodies.

He had older sisters, so he knew the most about sex, and he talked about it with a creativity that rivaled what I would later read in *Fanny Hill* and *The Marriage Art*.

That was what our group liked about him. But now this fount of sexual knowledge and obscene metaphors had suddenly dried up. Bruce's newfound piety elevated his obnoxiousness to a new level. At school, he tucked a King James New Testament in his shirt pocket and let the little ribbon in the Bible hang out so everyone knew what it was.

Before meals in the cafeteria, he closed his eyes, frowned, bowed his head, and clasped his forehead between his right forefinger and thumb before he took out his sandwich. He looked like he had a headache.

We excommunicated Bruce from our group, so during the summer of our shotgun bouts, he wasn't around to see Les put the safety back on his 12-gauge and step back in retreat.

But he had prayed for me all that year.

In August 1965, a year after our group shunned Bruce, I accepted his invitation to a Billy Graham crusade in Houston. The series of services drew 700,000 people. I went, not because I wanted to hear a sermon, but to see the biggest city in Texas and the world's first domed football stadium.

President Lyndon B. Johnson had flown in from his Texas ranch. The Astrodome swelled with 61,000 people—10,000 more than its capacity for a sporting event. The scoreboard lit up with the words JESUS SAID . . . 'I AM THE WAY . . . THE TRUTH . . . AND THE LIFE.'—JOHN 14.

I had no idea what that meant, and I didn't care, for Saint Peter's scales had long prevailed, staving off any serious consideration of God. At the end of his sermon, Billy Graham invited people to the front. I looked over at Bruce, who had one of his headaches.

My cheeks flushed. I felt that presence pull me forward, that same warmth I had felt in the church when I was eleven, the Sunday that God had waited for me down at the front of the church. I wanted this soft, inarticulate presence that called out to me gently enough that I could resist. I knew I should go to him. But I knew I could not shoulder the burden of Saint Peter's scales.

I stayed in my seat.

I didn't see Bruce again until three and a half months later. He talked me into spending a Friday night at his home with the promise of meeting some new girls the next day from Paschal High

School on Fort Worth's wealthy west side. He failed to mention that the girls wanted to be Christian missionaries.

Maybe being with Bruce again reminded me of the experience at the crusade. I'm not sure what prompted me, but on December 18, 1965, at 2 a.m., as I lay in bed in the dark, I asked Bruce how a person gets into heaven.

"You trust Jesus," he said. "Jesus died on the cross for you. He will forgive you, come into your heart, give you a new life, and never leave."

"That can't be true, Bruce," I said. "What if I do something bad later?"

"Jackie, you will do lots of bad things the rest of your life."

"But how do you know God will never leave me?"

"Jesus said so."

"Really?"

"Jesus said in John 10:28, 'I give my sheep eternal life, and they shall never perish; no one will snatch them out of my hand.'"

Bruce rolled over in his bed and went to sleep.

I stared at the ceiling as the promises rolled over me in waves: *He died for you. He will forgive you. He will give you new life.*

And the most important:

He will never leave you.

He will never leave you.

He will never leave you.

I let go of something inside me.

I believed.

The next morning, the meeting with the girls still waited, but I had forgotten to bring a fresh shirt. I dashed back to my house.

The day before, I had stolen six madras shirts and told Bobbie to iron them. But there they lay on my bed, still wrapped in cellophane. I snatched them up, stomped into the den where Bobbie ironed clothes. I threw the shirts on the kitchen counter.

"Bobbie, I told you to iron these damn shirts. Now I don't have anything to wear."

Without a word, she unwrapped a shirt and draped it over the ironing board.

I sulked back to my room. As I closed the door, I thought, *I can't talk like that anymore.* I said out loud, "I'm sorry, Lord."

Then I returned to the den.

"Bobbie, I'm sorry I got mad at you. Those shirts aren't important. I'll wear something else. I'm sorry I cussed. I don't want to use those words anymore."

She stood there speechless.

God was making himself at home in my heart, having slipped in through the crack of an open wound.

Eleven

I didn't tell Bruce what had happened right away because I didn't understand it myself. But after a few days, I called him. "I want to come over to God's side," I said.

"Don't go anywhere, Jackie. I'll be right over."

He showed up at my doorstep ten minutes later. We sat side by side on the couch in my living room. Bruce opened his King James Bible to John 3:3 and read, "Jesus answered and said unto him, 'Verily, verily, I say unto thee, Except a man be born again, he cannot see the kingdom of God.'"

"Jackie, you've been born again," he said. "You have become a spiritual baby in God's family. Now you have the rest of your life to grow up into a spiritual adult."

Bruce left his Bible with me and told me to read it and to pray. The Elizabethan English did not trouble me. It increased the holiness of the Bible. Every verse offered me the insight, beauty, and liberation that I had never experienced in any other book.

"Seek ye first the kingdom of God, and his righteousness; and all these things shall be added unto you," Jesus said in his Sermon on the Mount (Matthew 6:33).

I no longer had to steal my clothes.

But as Scripture cemented my transformation, I feared what I might have to give up in the transition from my old life to my new life.

I would be exiled, just like Bruce. Although I could stomach losing most of my friends, I feared that without Teddy and Philip, my new life would turn gray. The three of us had been bound by love, lust, drunkenness, and thievery. On some nights, we fogged up the windows of Teddy's '62 Chevy Impala, making out with our girlfriends and writing their names on those fogged-up windows.

Teddy and Philip had become the anchors of my self-worth.

I grew up in a home that had been robbed of love by some dark power that none of us understood. I would have said that Mom loved me, but it was a conditional, volcanic love. My brothers and I fought all the time. The girls came and went. But Teddy and Philip had been constants in my life since the seventh grade. What they gave me is what Nonnie gave me—unconditional love. In spite of my academic and athletic failures, their love proved to me that at least a part of me was valuable. I never told Philip or Teddy that they were the source of my main happiness. I never said to either of them, "I love you." Neither men nor boys talked like that in 1965 Texas.

Before word about me finding religion leaked out, I needed to do some damage control.

Philip, a blond, six-foot-four, all-star tight end, lived in the country on a few acres close to Lake Arlington, where I learned to ride horses, shoot guns, and water ski.

School was out for the Christmas holidays, so one sunny morning, Philip and I saddled up the horses. I pulled the cinch tight and said, "Philip, I have been born again."

"What?" he said.

"I've been born again. That's what Bruce said has happened to me."

"I knew I should never have let you go to hear Billy Graham with Bruce!"

"No, Philip. It wasn't Billy Graham. I just want to follow God now."

"Look, Jackie, I know all about religion. I went to the Baptist church out here until the seventh grade. A little religion is okay. But don't go overboard. Don't become a fanatic like Bruce."

"Don't worry, I won't."

That wasn't so bad. We were still solid, though we would never get drunk together again. Philip would never be my getaway driver again for my heists of expensive clothes.

The next night, I sat in Teddy's car in my driveway.

Teddy was a single-parent kid like me. He lived with his father and grew up in the country like Philip, but without any family money. What he lacked in wealth, he made up for in relational intelligence beyond his years. He was the most beloved kid in our class. Before Teddy, I had never witnessed anyone use self-deprecating humor. Teddy made himself the butt of every joke in a way that drew people to him, despite his out-of-style shirts and hand-me-down shoes.

"Teddy, I've given myself to God."

"What does that mean, Jackie?"

"It means I can't get drunk anymore, no more swearing, no more stealing, and no more feeling up girls."

"Sounds good to me."

What!

It didn't even sound good to me.

Twelve

Since I could not tell Teddy how to give himself to God, I took him to Bruce—the one-time fount of sexual knowledge had been reborn into a fount of theological knowledge. Before the year ran out, Teddy and I knelt side by side on the cold floor of my bedroom, and Teddy traded in his old life for the promise of God's new life.

In those first weeks of my new life, I sat alone on our living room couch and heard God speak to me in Elizabethan words from the King James Bible. After all the lights were out and my family was asleep, I turned on the stereo and listened to George Beverly Shea, Billy Graham's soloist. He sang "How Great Thou Art," and I cried. I couldn't have told anyone what I felt or why that feeling led to tears, but I knew the tears were good. I was worshiping, though I could not have told you what worship was.

After John 10:28, the most important verse, the verse that defined my life, was 2 Corinthians 5:17: "Therefore if any man be in Christ, he is a new creature: old things are passed away; behold, all things are become new."

That verse settled everything for me. My life before Christ had become irrelevant to my new life. Once I was bad, but now I will be good. I was bad because I had decided to be bad. Now I have decided to be good. That's what God wants, and it can't be that hard to be good since I am a new creature and since Jesus lives inside me. I no longer swore, drank, or stole. I did nothing more with girls than kiss. I was on the road to being a good person.

Bruce said that church was required in our new life. He took Teddy and me to our first church service at Sagamore Hill Baptist. We passed through the lobby and found our seats in the pew. It seemed as if I had crossed a border into another country.

In the auditorium, everyone was quiet. We sat on comfortable benches with gold cushions among a thousand other worshipers. The men wore coats and ties. The mothers and grandmothers wore fine dresses, and some wore hats and veils. Perfume wafted across the aisles, commingled with the scent of mothballs. The boys wore slacks and tucked-in shirts and loafers. The girls wore dresses—as far as I could tell, the same dresses they wore to school.

At eleven o'clock, the choir flowed in through doors from either side behind the stage. The two streams of white robes trimmed in gold crisscrossed as they filled a three-tier loft at the back of the stage. The choir director stood in the center of the stage with his back to the audience. When he raised his arms high, the organ boomed out the first notes. Then the piano and the choir joined in. I had never heard such music. After the songs and announcements, the pastor walked to the pulpit.

He stood six foot tall. A few extra pounds hung off his frame. The deep crevices under his eyes and his gray wavy hair made me think he was about sixty years old. His name was Fred Swank, but everybody referred to him as "Brother Swank." When he opened his Bible, people looked as if their grandfather was about to cuddle them, which was strange because he talked about hell and yelled.

His sermon was based on a passage from Luke's gospel. "As these things come to pass," Brother Swank said, "then *look up!* . . . and lift up your heads, for your redemption draweth nigh."

Brother Swank punctuated his main points by shouting *"look up"* throughout the whole sermon. Those main points sailed right over my head, for I didn't even know what a "point" was, and I never understood what good "looking up" would do for me.

Then Brother Swank prayed, revealing other curiosities. His

normal tone disappeared. The pitch of his voice rose and fell, again emphasizing certain words over others for no apparent reason, like a song without rhythm.

When he addressed God, he said "Thou" or "Thee" instead of you. It never became clear to me why God preferred antiquated second-person pronouns to modern ones. I learned three things about prayer that first Sunday: You can't use your normal voice to talk to God. You can't say "you" to God. And you can't talk to God with your eyes open.

After the prayer, Brother Swank told us if we wanted to get saved, to come forward. The choir sang, "Just as I am without one plea."

"This is the part where you go down to the front," whispered Bruce.

Teddy and I slipped out of our pew and walked forward to the strains of "Just as I Am" and in full view of the shocked stares of the kids we had once regarded as the social lepers of our high school—the nice kids with no personality. Another minister wrote down our names, phone numbers, and addresses.

At the end of the service, Brother Swank read our names from the pulpit and encouraged the congregation to join us at the altar so they could offer us the "right hand of fellowship"—what Southern Baptists at that time called a handshake.

Teddy and I had now become citizens of this strange new country.

Every Sunday morning and evening and every Wednesday night, we sang hymns and listened to the same five or six sermons over and over. I liked it. For the first time, there was order in my life.

I was welcomed into the families of my new friends. I always had a place to eat a great Sunday lunch—fried chicken and mashed potatoes with creamy gravy, or pot roasts, like we used to have when Dad was alive. I saw stable fathers who kissed their wives in public.

Within six months, I had read the entire Bible. In Sunday school at Sagamore Baptist, I listened to the teacher describe stories I already knew by heart. He could not ask a question to which I didn't know the answer.

Dad never bragged on me, but men in the church did. Mr. Kliever, the superintendent of the eleventh-grade Sunday school department, said to me, "You have only been a Christian a short time, but you know the Bible better than all these kids who have been here their entire lives."

Even more than tithing—giving 10 percent of our income to God—Brother Swank stressed witnessing to our friends and even to strangers.

So I invited Bill, who had accompanied me to the Mexican whorehouse, to spend a Saturday night at my house. Bill's rich girlfriend had dumped him for an older, sleazy guy. Bill was ripe for salvation.

"We don't have much time, Bill," I said in my bedroom. "The Russians will kill us in a nuclear war, or Jesus will come back soon and destroy the earth. Either way, if you don't give yourself to Jesus, you will go to hell."

"I'm not sure," Bill said.

"Not sure about what?" I asked.

"I just don't feel ready," Bill said.

How could he not be ready?

In the ninth grade, I witnessed a 140-pound Bill pummel a 250-pound bully named Clifford. Clifford managed to land one good punch, but it just glanced off Bill's jaw. Bill wrestled the bully to the ground, sat astride his chest, and beat his face bloody. Bill stopped and said, "Clifford, I can do this all day long. Do you give up?"

Clifford gave up.

That night, I pummeled Bill with one hellish scenario after another in order to scare him into the kingdom.

At 2 a.m., Bill gave up.

"All right. I'll pray the damn prayer," Bill said.

I had him kneel with me beside my bed and told him what to pray.

"Now can we go to bed?" Bill asked.

"Sure, but we have to go to church in the morning," I said.

I dragged Bill to the 8:15 a.m. service the next morning. At the end, the choir began "Just as I Am."

I leaned over and whispered to Bill, "This is the part where you go down to the front."

"I'm not ready."

"What do you mean you're not ready?"

"Jackie, I just don't want to do it now."

"Bill, you got saved last night. You have to go."

"I'm not going."

"Hypocrite."

Thirteen

I wanted to be an executive at General Motors like Dad. But when Dad killed himself, he killed my plan for my life. Since there would be no money for college, there was no reason for school. And no teacher had ever showed me the utility of math, the purpose of history, or the beauty of Shakespeare.

So I passed on school and searched for beauty in novels and movies. The novels and movies did not offer me a plan for my life, but they did give a dream for happiness on earth. In these stories, the good guy always beat the bad guy, and his reward was the beautiful girl. The kiss came at the end of the movie. The kiss meant that the battle was won and nothing was left to do except ride off into the sunset together and enjoy happily ever after. The movie ended, but the kiss went on forever and ever.

I grew up in the world of The Kiss, not the world of the blow job.

The Kiss gave me hope that my life would not turn out like my parents' lives. The Kiss helped me get out of bed after nightmares of seeing Dad burning in the caverns of hell. The Kiss carried me as I carried drunken Mom to her bed at night.

I watched The Kiss over and over.

Night after night, I dreamed of The Kiss that would make me forever happy. I dreamed of falling in love with a beautiful girl, whom I would not touch until our wedding launched us into ecstasy. Forever.

I listened to romantic ballads by Roy Orbison and Ray Charles as I fell asleep. I fantasized the most beautiful girl in my class right into my marriage bed.

In the seventh grade, her name was Fawn. Perfect for a boy named Deere. She was not only the most beautiful girl in my class, she was also the sweetest. But she didn't love me. Some nights when I thought of us lying naked in bed together, I listened to Ray sing, "You don't know me . . . For I never knew the art of making love, though my heart aches with love for you. Afraid and shy, I let my chance go by."

"Afraid and shy." Ray sang my story. Yet I clung to my fantasy.

Then I saw her.

She looked like a Cherokee princess, black hair with subtle auburn strands and perfect, tanned skin with the faintest red undertones.

It was a Saturday afternoon in downtown Fort Worth. I stood transfixed in the lobby of the Hollywood Theatre. It was May 1963. *Dr. No*, the first James Bond movie, had opened. In a few moments, I would see Ursula Andress come up out of the sea in a white bikini. But Ursula could not compare to the beautiful girl I stared at in that lobby laughing with her three girlfriends.

"Did you see her?" I asked Bruce.

"Forget about her. Her name is Charlotte. She's a cheerleader for Meadowbrook Junior High. She's a church girl. She would never go out with you."

She was only fifteen feet away, but my legs were paralyzed. I did not try to meet her, not because she was a church girl, but because someone that beautiful was out of my class. Girls never said I was handsome. I was consigned to being cute, if I were consigned at all.

Roy Orbison sang that love hurts. Maybe for him, but I did not believe love would hurt me. Love was ecstasy, not pain. Yet it hurt to know that my forever girl would never look this good. I was fourteen years old.

I ran through a few girlfriends in high school before I crashed into God and landed at Charlotte's church. I asked her out. She said yes.

Our first kisses were sweet, not passionate. I had wanted one thing from all the girls in my old life: sex. In my new life, I simply wanted her. Like Elvis's forlorn lament, she was always on my mind.

Holding her hand was more intoxicating than any sexual adventure I'd had with other girls. Seeing what might just be love for me in those brown eyes skyrocketed my self-esteem.

One Sunday morning, we stood to sing "Count Your Blessings." She said, "This is my favorite hymn." The hymn had been published in 1897. The hymn's melody had not stood the test of time. It sounded like an advertising jingle. The first stanza went like this:

When upon life's billows you are tempest-tossed,
When you are discouraged, thinking all is lost,
Count your many blessings—name them one by one,
And it will surprise you what the Lord hath done.

I was proud of the goodness and sweetness of the rock & roll girl who could love bad music for the purity of its theology. The song extolled her approach to life: dwell on the good with a thankful heart, even when the storm is about to take you down. Charlotte never laid a word of blame on anyone.

Then came our first crisis.

Charlotte's old flame was coming back to town. He was a magnificent athlete with a body that Apollo would envy. One girl told me he used to dive off the roof of her house into the swimming pool, a feat no other boy had attempted. He would be in town for a single Friday night. I could not compete with a Greek god, nor could I forbid her to see him. So I asked her out for the one Friday night when he would be in town. She said yes. Disaster averted.

In those days, no self-respecting girl in Fort Worth would ever call a boy on the phone. When I picked up the phone and heard her voice on Thursday afternoon, I knew my plan had backfired.

"Jackie, someone I used to date will be in town for only this Friday night, and he wants to see me. Would you mind if we changed our date to another night?" she asked.

I would rather have walked barefoot on hot coals and broken glass all the way to downtown Dallas than let her go out with Apollo. My forever-after happiness was at stake. So I did what always came naturally to me in a crisis.

I lied.

"No, of course not. Go, have fun. We'll see each other next weekend or whenever we can," I said.

"Thanks for understanding," she said.

"Sure. Bye."

"Bye."

I hated that black rotary dial telephone for betraying me. Before that call, I loved everyone in the world. I had not a single enemy. I had forgiven everyone. The magic in my girlfriend had exalted me to a new, happy version of life. I hated Roy Orbison for being right. Love did hurt. My soul spent Friday night in lower Hades, imagining my girlfriend with Apollo.

A week later, she resurrected me. We were back on our normal schedule. We did not talk about Apollo until later.

One evening in late spring, we sat in my car in front of my house. I pulled her to me to kiss her.

"If you kiss me, you'll get my horrible cold," she warned.

"I'm happy to share your cold," I said.

A few minutes later, we paused, and she said the magic words, "I love you."

"I love you too," I said back.

"I was so worried when you were so calm about me breaking the date with you to see my old boyfriend. I thought you didn't care at all."

"Of course I cared, but I would never let you see it. I asked you out for that Friday night to prevent you from seeing him."

I would not confess to my night in Hades. I thought if she knew how much power she had over me, she might not want me as much.

In August, Charlotte and I went to Sagamore's church camp about ninety miles south of Fort Worth. The sulfuric water stank. You could drink it, provided you were dying of thirst. We slept thirty to a dormitory with no air-conditioning in the Texas heat. In the morning, they served us cold, powdered scrambled eggs. The girls had the pool for the first two hours of the afternoon. The boys had it for the last two hours, and we could not come to the pool until a counselor made sure the last girl had left. At night, we went to a "revival meeting" in an open-air tabernacle, where a guest preacher preached salvation to the saved.

Mr. Kliever, my favorite deacon, gave up one week of his vacation to chaperone the youth camp in the summer.

"Mr. Kliever, is it okay to kiss Charlotte at church camp?" I asked.

"If you do, make sure you kiss her where nobody can see," he smiled back.

That answer had two different possible interpretations. I don't think the one I preferred would have occurred to him.

As a new convert, I was asked to give my testimony, the story of my conversion to Christ, to the couple hundred campers at the evening revival service. I told them about Dad, about my stealing, and about Bruce reaching out to me. I ended my talk with 2 Corinthians 6:10: "As sorrowful, yet always rejoicing; as poor, yet making many rich; as having nothing, and yet possessing all things."

I explained how each clause applied to my life. I said that if you have God, you have everything. Some said it was the best testimony they had ever heard.

All the boys met in a grove and sat on stones one afternoon to pray for the evening meeting. Brother Swank said, "Some of you boys aren't walking with the Lord like you know you should be. I want every head bowed, every eye closed. If you're not walking with the Lord like you could be, raise your hand. I want to pray for you."

As boys raised their hands, Brother Swank would say, "I see that hand. I'll pray for you."

I could witness more, I thought. *I could read the Bible more. I could pray more. I waste too much time.*

I raised my hand.

"I won't accept that hand," Brother Swank said.

I put it down.

Before camp ended, I was given the "Best Camper" award, along with a small, red New Testament inscribed with the words "Best Camper Sagamore Hill 1966."

Maybe God needed me, I thought. I was proof that his church provided a life superior to the life of sin and that anyone could change.

———

One afternoon, Charlotte and I skipped our separate pool times and went for an afternoon walk hand in hand along a deep, dry riverbed. I found an overhanging ledge seven feet high. I checked for wasps, scorpions, and snakes before we slipped under it, sat down, held each other, and kissed. After a few minutes, we heard the high-pitched voices of junior high boys as they walked above us toward the edge of the ledge. I put my finger on her lips to signal absolute silence.

There were three or four different voices above us. Then we heard their zippers come down. The boys decided to have a contest over our ledge. Yellow streams rained down. Most of them cleared the ledge. But some didn't and splashed close to our feet.

We choked back the laughter.

Under a wall of urine, I held fast to my forever girl and to the belief that my willpower would keep us pure.

Fourteen

At the end of a Wednesday night church service in March 1966, a man with short black hair and an olive complexion walked down the aisle toward me. He was about my height, but nine years older. He wore a black golf shirt that stretched tight over his biceps. Veins rippled across his forearms—tributaries carved from his college wrestling days.

"Hi," he said, "my name is Scott Manley."

"I'm Jackie Deere."

"I know. I've heard about you. You sound like an interesting guy. I lead the Young Life club at Richland High School."

"What's Young Life?"

"Why don't you come with me next Monday night and find out?"

The next Monday night, Scott came to my house and met Mom. Then we headed for Richland Hills, a middle-class suburb a little newer and nicer than mine. The house teemed with the laughter of teenagers. The various layers of the social strata at Richland High School were all represented—the athletes revered as gods and the cheerleader goddesses, the hoods who wore black jackets and smoked, the math geeks who carried slide rules for calculus, and the indistinguishables still searching for identity.

Scott had made friends of all of them.

At 7:30, he shouted, "Time to get started." In the living room, the furniture had been pushed back to the wall. One hundred twenty-five kids sat squashed together on the floor. We sang rowdy spiritual songs and watched a skit that brought howls of laughter.

Scott congratulated the football team for Friday night's victory. He praised the wide receiver for a spectacular catch that sealed the win, but then mocked him for posing for a sideline photographer as a safety knocked him out of bounds. The kids laughed and shouted at the receiver and slapped him on the back.

Then Scott talked about a God who liked us, whether we were drunk or sober, pure or impure, whether we made A's or F's—not an authoritarian deity who would drown you in a swimming hole for skipping church.

As he closed in prayer, some kids wiped tears from their eyes. It was over in an hour, but everyone lingered.

In my bed that night, I thought about what I had just witnessed. Since Dad had died, the only heroes in my life were Steve McQueen, Sean Connery, and Clint Eastwood. I still carried a razor blade in my billfold so if a bad guy jumped me in the bathroom like the bad guy who jumped Steve in *The Cincinnati Kid*, I could humiliate him with a razor blade to the throat. For the first time since Dad threw me away, I had a real-life hero. I wanted to win hearts like Scott. I wanted his happiness and his speaking ability, and most of all, I longed for his confidence, because a boy without confidence just stumbles through his life feeling like a mistake.

The next week, Scott asked, "Do you want to play handball this Saturday morning?"

Of course I wanted to play handball. Handball was a college boy's game, a sign of stature and sophistication. But the high schools didn't have handball courts. Scott took me to a gym just south of downtown that had two handball courts and taught me the one sport that I would become good at in my youth.

Afterward, we went to breakfast in our soaked T-shirts and gym shorts at the Ol' South Pancake House on University Drive. We finished the pancakes and whipped out our Bibles. I was already reading the Bible like Jesus was coming back next week to give me a test on Scripture. That morning, Scott taught me to study the Bible. We turned to 2 Timothy.

"Jackie, the paragraph, not the verse, is the unit of study. Boil each paragraph down to its essence. Give it a three-word title—subject, verb, and object. Then memorize all your titles, and you will have 2 Timothy down," he said. Within a few days, I could close my eyes and think my way through all four chapters of 2 Timothy. Then we studied 1 Peter. Storing books of Scripture on the shelves of my brain turned into a lifelong pleasure.

Those Saturday morning handball matches gave back a sensation I hadn't experienced in years—the feeling of being valued by somebody I worshiped. I could confess almost anything to Scott, even if it made me feel like a fake Christian.

I asked Scott what he thought about masturbation. He told me that a prominent Christian writer had deemed it a gift from God. Scott's view was that "it's normal, but not the best thing for you."

I knew that it increased my lust rather than diminished it, especially considering what went through my mind. Then there was the guilt and embarrassment that accompanied it. I felt defeated after it was over.

And then there was the ultimate purpose of the orgasm—a reward for love, not a pleasure to be turned in on yourself. I swore off masturbation completely.

I had a bigger problem than masturbation to talk over with Scott.

"I don't like prayer," I said to Scott.

I explained that each night, I waited for my two brothers to fall asleep. Then I slid out of my covers, knelt beside my bed on the floor, shivered in my Fruit of the Loom underwear, and tried to figure out what you say to a person who knows everything and who never seems to talk back. My mind wandered all over the cold night in a fruitless search for words to warm my heart and please my new God.

"Use ACTS to organize your prayers," said Scott.

"You mean the book of the Bible?"

"No, it's an acronym. A-C-T-S.

"The *A* is for Adoration. Tell God how wonderful he is. It gives God pleasure to hear you celebrate your experience of his wisdom, power, and love, and it awakens more of your love for him. We praise everything we love, for praise completes our enjoyment of what we love.

"The *C* is for Confession. Jackie, you will sin until the day God takes you to heaven. The softer your heart becomes, the greater your sins will seem, and the more painful your guilt will feel. Tell God you're sorry for your sin, and he will release you from the prison of your guilt. You can never deserve or earn forgiveness. It is a gift that Jesus bought for us on his cross. All we have to do to receive that gift is confess our sin and trust him for his forgiveness.

"The *T* is for Thanksgiving. Thank God for the big blessings every day—for his love, for your new life, for forgiveness—but also look for new things each day to thank him for. Grateful children make their heavenly Father happy."

That was a staggering mystery: someone as imperfect as me could make a perfect Person happy.

"The *S* is for Supplication. Pray for others and yourself. Be specific. Nothing is too small or too big to ask for. Even though God already knows what we need, he wants us to ask for our needs and desires. It gives him pleasure to hear us ask for help, and it increases our faith when he gives us exactly the help we asked for. If God doesn't give us what we ask for, it's because our timing is wrong or because he wants to give us something better."

He said, "Remember, Jackie, prayer is what makes life work." Then Scott prayed with me in the same voice and with the same vocabulary he used to teach me handball. And he prayed with me often. And I came to enjoy praying, though not as much as I enjoyed studying the Bible.

One Saturday morning, we sat in the bleachers waiting for one of the handball courts to open up. Scott handed me four cards the size of business cards. They each had a Bible verse printed on the card, with the reference of the verse printed at the bottom and the topic of the verse printed at the top. It was the Navigators topical memory system. Scott told me that if I wanted to know God, I would have to memorize individual verses of Scripture. For it is God's Word hidden in our hearts that revives our soul, makes us wise, rejoices our heart, gives light to our eyes, and enables us to walk in purity (Psalm 19:7–8; 119:9, 11). I didn't know that my soul needed reviving, but I did what Scott told me to do anyway.

Before I graduated from high school, I had memorized the whole system, 144 verses, letter-perfect, in King James English. And then I added to the system, making my own cards.

Reading, studying, memorizing, and meditating on Scripture gave me pleasure like listening to music.

Scott showed me where I went wrong "witnessing" to Bill.

"Jackie, your anger was the sign that you did not love or respect Bill. You tried to collect a trophy so you could feel better about yourself," Scott said.

He told me that witnessing was loving people and telling them the story of our experience of God's love.

"Tell people what your life was like before you knew Jesus, how you met Jesus, and how your life is different now," said Scott.

Then he took me to Richland High to tell my story to a group of guys who met with him on Wednesday mornings at 6:30 to study the Bible before school. There were twelve guys. After I finished, the quarterback spoke for all the guys when he said, "Cool story, man!"

Scott took me to breakfast.

"Jackie, you did fantastic," he said.

"Really?"

"I've heard a lot of people tell their story. Your story is one of the most powerful stories I've ever heard. And you told it so well."

My heart soared on that praise. It was better than my fantasy of scoring the winning touchdown after the clock had run out.

Fifteen

The summer before my senior year, Scott took me to a weeklong Young Life camp nestled in the Colorado mountains. I tried to take along the girl who was the undoing and remaking of my world, but her rich father wouldn't let her go. He thought Young Life was a Communist organization bent on overthrowing the church he never attended.

Besides the most fun I'd ever had in my entire life, I heard Christian speakers talk about the two subjects that dominated most teenagers' minds: love and sex.

"Being in love is the greatest feeling in the world," said Arnie Jacobs, one of Young Life's most polished speakers. "When I fell in love with Mary Lou, I couldn't think about anything else except her. Then we married, and the craziness of 'in love' left. If it hadn't, I would never have gotten anything done."

I didn't buy it. He's just old. I was too special for a marriage like that.

After that meeting, I talked to a fortysomething, five-foot-two, dark-haired woman counselor. I was intrigued by the fact that she had been a missionary in some far-off country. She took an interest in the kid who could spout Scripture, quote C. S. Lewis by the yard, and talked too fast to have a Texas drawl.

"I will never sin again sexually," I vowed.

"Oh no, Jackie, don't ever say that," she said.

"Don't say what?"

"Don't say you'll never commit another sexual sin."

"Well, I won't. I know I won't."

"That's pride, Jackie."

"It's not pride. It's a plan, and it works. I have the most beautiful girl in the world, and all we do is kiss. And that's all we will do until we marry."

The missionary and I changed subjects. At the end of the week, I came home to my Cherokee princess.

Charlotte's father owned his own business. They had a beautiful home in Eastern Hills. The house had expensive Early American furniture, wool carpets, rich wood paneling, and nothing out of place. The backyard was landscaped with tall oak trees and a swimming pool. I had never been in a home like hers. All of my friends lived in houses that reflected the damage our fathers and mothers had done to each other.

At the end of the summer, we swam in her pool in the moonlight. She said, "I feel like I've always known you."

"I know. I feel the same way, but there is one thing about me you don't know," I said.

I told her about the Mexican whorehouse. She was relieved. She thought I had a huge sexual history that featured many girls. Until that moment, I had regretted the absence of such an expansive history in my past. Now I was glad I didn't have an album of naked bodies in my memory to compete with hers.

Under the full moon, we held each other in waist-deep water. I kissed the droplets off her neck and shoulder. My hands stayed on her back. But the swimsuits, the skin on skin, the moonlight and the pressure of her body against mine cranked my desire right to the limit of my resistance.

I had to keep our love legal, or I would lose it. If my hands or lips crossed the boundaries of purity, I would betray the God who had given me this wonderful girl to love. If I touched her in the secret places, I would disrespect her. If I disrespected her, it would mean I didn't love her or God. And I would lose her.

In the spring of our senior year, I bought her a tiny golden heart necklace. The heart was woven with two layers of gold strands to make it look like gold rope. At the top of the heart on the bottom of the V was a speck of diamond.

I picked her up on her birthday while it was still light. When we were away from her house, I stopped the car and gave her the necklace.

"Oh!" she gasped. "My first diamond!" She looked at it for a moment and then said, "I don't think I can keep it."

"What do you mean?" I asked.

"My parents may not let me," she said.

"Well, don't show it to your parents," I said.

I had read the Ten Commandments. I knew we were supposed to honor our fathers and mothers. But at that moment, what I felt for my girl had more authority over me than God's Ten Commandments. She kept the diamond.

We graduated in 1967 at the end of May. Philip's dad bought him a brand-new Oldsmobile 442. We decided to break the muscle car in on a road trip to Southern California. We had friends and relatives there, so we had plenty of places to stay. We set a day to leave, but no day to return.

On the day of our departure, Philip and Kathy, his cheerleader girlfriend, picked me up. Then we picked up Charlotte, who would spend the night at Kathy's house after Philip and I left for California.

At 11 p.m., we changed into our swimsuits for a moonlight swim in the lake. Charlotte came out of the house in a new one-piece swimsuit, brown trimmed in blue. Philip whistled when he saw her.

"Man, you look beautiful!" he said.

And she did. We never made it to the water. Philip and Kathy went somewhere else, while we went to the backseat.

I had never wanted anything or anyone as much as I wanted her that night. It felt like we were merging into one person, both wanting each other with all our hearts. We took each other into a new realm of desire. I wanted to take her swimsuit off, and I knew she hoped that I would. That night was a thousand times more sensual than the night with the Mexican prostitute. It was supposed to be. We were in love. We were on fire. I wanted her, but not in the backseat. I would not reduce her to a conquest. I wanted her forever, not just for this night. So I made myself stop while I could.

My will won out against my desire that night, but that night had created a video in my mind that would bludgeon my will all the way to the California coast.

After she'd had time to reflect on that night, Charlotte thanked me for stopping when she didn't want to stop. She said I had contradicted everything she had been told about boys. Boys take everything they can get, and when they can't get any more, they leave. She said she loved me more than ever and trusted me completely.

At 1:30 a.m., Charlotte and Kathy stood in the street and waved good-bye to us. I turned to watch her through the rear window until the night took her away from me. I didn't want to leave her, but I resigned myself to the trip and settled into the front seat of the 442. As soon as we hit the highway, Philip had the car up to 100 mph. We drove like the devil was chasing us.

I missed her every mile. And I couldn't get my mind out of that backseat. The video in my mind kept me in a constant state of arousal and fantasy. I wished I had stayed in the backseat longer. I could not wait to climb back in.

The next evening, I stood on the pier at Huntington Beach, and for the first time, I watched the star that the ancients had worshiped drop into the ocean, and I worshiped the God who painted the sky orange and purple and gave me someone more beautiful than the sunset to love. I felt the pain of her absence. She should have been there beside me. My arm should have been around her. We should have shared the beauty of that first ocean sunset together. All of our firsts should be together from now on.

In the days that followed that sunset, I replayed and fantasized our last night together nonstop, and each day the fever grew—until I masturbated.

I confessed my sin to God, but I still felt ruined.

The smile of the Father who would never leave me had vanished. All I could see was the scowl of a disappointed taskmaster.

Sixteen

A letter from Charlotte arrived the next day. On the outside of the envelope, she had drawn a biplane flying through the clouds and written "Air Mail" in different colors of ink, along with the phrase, "O fly it to him!" In that letter, she pleaded with me to come home.

I didn't answer her letter. I let her wonder when I was coming home.

I returned to Texas from California in the middle of June, but left two weeks later to spend all of July at the Young Life camp in Colorado. I did not call Charlotte or answer her letters.

Late in the summer, Bruce warned me.

"She's bitter," he said.

———————

At the end of August 1967, on a whim and a last-minute student loan and grant, courtesy of Lyndon Baines Johnson's Great Society, I left Scott Manley and followed Charlotte to Texas Tech University. I went three hundred miles west of Fort Worth to the bleak, windblown prairies of West Texas.

The first Monday on campus, I asked Charlotte out for Friday night. She already had plans. She already had plans for Saturday night too. She was booked for the rest of September. I refused to stand in line for her.

Crawling, I thought, *is the quickest way to lose her forever.* So

I considered myself dumped on a warm, sunny September afternoon. I smiled at her as though my heart did not hurt, as though the world were still right. I said good-bye and watched the only girl I had ever loved leave me. As she disappeared into her dorm, I resolved never to call her or try to see her again. Her first week at college had taught her what I had known all along: my beautiful girl could do so much better than to settle for a poor, insecure boy who had no plan for his life.

With romance out of the way, I told myself I might as well salvage my college experience with an education.

In an auditorium with a hundred other students, I wondered if I could make it through Botany, rumored to be the hardest freshman class. The professor, a short, redheaded woman, announced in a monotone voice, "Your grade will be determined by two tests—the midterm and the final. The questions will come from your assigned reading."

After a few weeks, I discovered that class attendance was superfluous. I had been scared into reading the Botany textbook, and I found that I could understand the book and that the teacher's lectures contributed nothing that wasn't already in the book.

The week before the midterm, I had read and outlined the first half of my Botany book. I spent two hours a day for several days before the exam memorizing my outline until I had it down letter-perfect. The exam was multiple choice, and I aced it in half the allotted time.

So halfway through my first freshman semester, I learned the principle that would allow me to coast through the boredom of higher academia: thinking is not required to do well on tests, only memorization. God had given me broad shoulders and a good memory. And I had been strengthening my memory ever since Scott Manley put the first four Navigator Scripture memory verse cards into my palm. As for thinking, C. S. Lewis taught me that.

In my English Literature class, I sat on the front row next to a brunette named Anne. Three times a week, we talked before and after class for a few minutes. We shared stories about our high school experiences in Houston and Fort Worth. She pressured her upperclassman Phi Delta boyfriend to invite me to a Phi Delta rush party. I embarrassed myself trying to produce interesting small talk by quoting things I had learned about Japanese culture from the latest James Bond novel. I had neither the looks nor money to impress any of the members. I had no high school athletic experience to contribute to the fraternity's athletic teams.

On Monday, Anne waved me to the seat next to her.

"So," she began, "how did the party go last weekend?"

"I didn't get an invitation to the party tonight. They must have scratched me off the list," I replied.

"Oh, no," her face fell. "I'm sorry, Jackie."

I lived in an athletic dorm, Bledsoe Hall. My dorm mates described in detail their encounters with prostitutes across the border or the porn films they had seen over the weekend.

I wanted to watch pornography, but C. S. Lewis had scared me away from porn. He defined addiction with a single sentence: "An ever increasing craving for an ever diminishing pleasure is the formula."[1]

So I passed on porn and played poker with the scholarship football players.

Now that romance, education, and fraternities were out of the way, I thought I'd salvage my college experience in the weight room. I lifted hard three days a week. I gained twenty pounds by the end of my first year, but my pants size stayed the same. I learned a harsh lesson in the Tech weight room: only losers went to the weight room on Friday nights. Everybody else went out—while I worked on a body that nobody wanted.

---

1. C. S. Lewis: *The Screwtape Letters: Annotated Edition* (1942; repr., San Francisco: HarperOne, 2013), 53.

I was so lonely that I went home once a month while I was at Tech, and the same thing happened every time.

Scott Manley would call and say, "Let's go out for dinner and a movie."

"I'd love to, but I don't have money for either. I used up my money for the gas to get home."

"No problem. I have plenty, and I'm happy to pay."

Every weekend I went home, I always went out with Scott.

I had chosen to spend the next four years three hundred miles away from Scott. I couldn't help him build a Young Life club or recruit workers for him from a local university. Yet there he was, waiting for me every time I came home.

Scott and I talked about almost everything. I talked to him about Scripture, about theology, about my forlorn love life, about everything except my masturbation. I was happy when I was with him.

I felt loved apart from my usefulness. Then the weekend would end, and I dragged myself back to my Tech misery.

Back at Tech, I walked alone from class to class. I watched couples stroll together arm in arm. Girls hurried along in groups and laughed. Guys joked and shoved each other. Everybody was with somebody except for me. I searched the student traffic for the faces of beautiful girls on their way to class—girls I wouldn't have had the guts to talk to—but I rarely saw a beautiful girl. I doubt that Tech was so bereft of beauty. It was only my girlfriend—former girlfriend—who made it seem so.

Early in the spring semester, I looked out my dorm window and saw buildings and people disappear as a one-hundred-foot-high wall of brown dust rolled into the campus. That dust was a perfect image of my miserable, barren, lightweight life at Tech.

What am I doing here?

That question shook me out of my stupor, and I decided to shake off the dust of Tech. My life was back in Fort Worth with Scott Manley and Young Life. I applied to Texas Christian University. TCU was the home of Slingin' Sammy Baugh and Davey O'Brien, two of the greatest quarterbacks in college football history. I was accepted and given the student loan and grant I needed to attend the much more expensive private school.

Until the very end of the spring semester, it looked like all I would take home was some extra muscle and a heavy GPA.

The week before spring finals, Charlotte's girlfriend intercepted me on the way to class. She told me Charlotte was failing Latin.

"Jackie, could you please help her? She is so scared," her friend implored.

Of course I would help her with Latin. I did not resent her for dumping me. Had I been her, I never would have picked me up.

I picked her up in the afternoon. It was the first time I had seen her in nine months. We went to the home of a Lubbock family that had befriended me. We went down to the basement and shut the door. She hadn't brought her Latin textbook—she wasn't failing Latin. Before she could say, *Ego amo te*, we were kissing. For the first time, my hand crossed the boundary that I had set to contain our love. And she let my hand rove. I caressed her out of the desire to mark her as mine. When we stopped kissing, she rested her head on my chest and cried softly.

"Why are you crying?" I asked.

"I've never done that before," she said.

I stroked her hair and said, "Good. I'm glad it was with me. All our firsts should be together from now on."

Seventeen

The endless romance promised by The Kiss was in reach again. But now I had a clear path back to Scott and Young Life in Fort Worth.

The Kiss would make me happy, I knew that, but could it give me purpose? And who did I want to be with more: the person I most wanted to possess, or the person I most wanted to be like?

I chose the latter.

That summer Scott and I had lunch by the pool at Colonial Country Club, where I had been given a job as a lifeguard.

"Jackie," he said, "you'll be with me at Richland High this year. I'll teach you how to give messages and train you to be a Young Life leader. Next year, I'll start a club at Arlington Heights High School, and you'll take over Richland High, so recruit a team from TCU this year to work with you."

"And one other thing. Guy Owen will work with us."

"Guy Owen?" I said. "I don't like Guy Owen."

"Jackie, you will love Guy Owen."

The reasons I didn't like Guy had more to do with me than him. During my junior year of high school on a bus to a Young Life camp in Colorado, I watched Guy lean over to Scott and point to a girl in the front.

"Do you know her name?" Guy asked.

"No," Scott said, "but I'll find out."

Scott got up and walked halfway down the aisle.

"Hey, what's your name?" Scott asked the girl, who was bewildered by the sudden attention from a male camp counselor.

"Sally," she said.

"Thanks," Scott said, as he turned to head back toward Guy.

Then in a voice loud enough for the entire bus to hear Scott announced, "It's Sally, Guy! She said her name is Sally."

The bus burst out with laughter so loud that it drowned out the sound of the diesel engine.

Any other boy would have been humiliated. But Guy sauntered right up to her. He spent the next couple of hours surrounded by Sally and her friends.

I said that I didn't like Guy because he was a show-off, but I lied to myself. I was jealous of him.

I gazed out the Greyhound's window at the cactus of the northern New Mexico desert as it faded into the red cedars at the foot of the Rockies, and I longed for that kind of confidence.

Three years later, Guy showed me around the TCU campus and took me to lunch.

"What does your father do?" I asked him.

"He's in charge of all the purchasing at Texas Instruments, but he'll never become a vice president because he didn't go to college," said Guy.

"Are you close to your dad?" I asked.

"No, not really," Guy said. "What does your dad do?"

"He killed himself when I was twelve years old," I said.

"That must have been terrible."

"It was hard on us. We almost lost our house twice because Mom couldn't pay the taxes. But that's all in the past. That old life is irrelevant now. Right?"

"Yes, of course," he said. "But I can't imagine growing up without a father."

Guy's confidence had made him one of the most popular figures on campus, and as it became clear that he wanted to be my friend, I changed my opinion of him. I traded in my jealousy for gratitude. I celebrated the gifts in Guy that I would never have.

Soon we registered for classes together.

Scott and Guy became fixtures at the country club pool where I worked. And Scott jump-started our training with summer Young Life meetings for three high schools in a downtown Fort Worth hotel.

Guy led the singing. He didn't have the greatest voice. But he could sing on key. And he injected humor into a space considered sacred. High school kids howled when he sang hymns in the voice of Joe Cocker. He imitated the singer's gyrations years before John Belushi incorporated the spastic movements into a skit on *Saturday Night Live*.

At the end of the summer, Scott and I drove his Volkswagen Beetle to a Young Life's Castaway Camp on a lake in Minnesota. The camp featured waterskiing and sailing. Scott was the head counselor, and I lived in a cabin with a different group of kids each week as their counselor.

I looked forward to taking over Scott's club. With him to guide me, I had nothing to fear. My life was back on track. But just before our sophomore classes started, I got a phone call.

"I need you and Guy to come over this afternoon," Scott said.

When Guy and I walked into Scott's one-room garage apartment, he had us sit on a bench in his kitchen on either side of him. Our backs were against the wall.

"Bob Mitchell called me today," Scott said. Mitchell was vice president of Young Life. I dreaded the next sentence.

"He wants me to move to Oklahoma City to become the area director," Scott said.

"But you don't have to go, do you?" I asked.

"I do if I want to stay with Young Life."

The three of us wept.

Why had God let Young Life yank the most irreplaceable person in my life to another state? There was no good answer.

But I couldn't shake my fist at God. He had given me eighteen months with a man who embodied Christ more than anyone I could imagine.

The boy who could not cry over the death of his father now wept over the loss of a friend.

Eighteen

A few months after I had become a believer, I lay down on my twin bed next to a window and opened the book that Scott had given me—C. S. Lewis's *The Screwtape Letters*. With each paragraph, my heart beat a little faster. The book contains a series of letters written by Screwtape, a senior demon, to Wormwood, a junior tempter. Wormwood's "patient" is a young man in Britain during World War II.

"Keep everything hazy in his mind now, and you will have all eternity wherein to amuse yourself by producing in him the peculiar kind of clarity which Hell affords," Screwtape advised Wormwood.[1]

That sentence transported me out of my drab bedroom into a realm of beauty and intellectual precision. It compressed the hatred of demonic strategy into a mere twenty-nine words.

I memorized it on my first reading with no effort.

Screwtape ruined me. I could no longer imagine myself navigating the corporate pecking order at General Motors. I wanted to spend the rest of my life contemplating eternal questions.

In church, I had received oblique warnings about the dangers of college philosophy. It could turn a lifelong believer into an apostate. But those admonitions made the world of Kant and Camus more attractive.

Before I stepped onto a college campus, I had already decided

---

1. Lewis, *Screwtape Letters*, 11.

to major in philosophy—an area of study that imperiled my faith and offered bleak prospects of a paycheck.

I had embraced the Christian faith as truth. That truth had set me free. Would it crumble under scrutiny? I had to find out.

As a nineteen-year-old sophomore at TCU, I swam in a sea of kids who drove new Buick Grand Sports and Pontiac GTOs, wore slacks and Bass Weejuns, and ate at restaurants with waiters in tuxedos.

They taught me about trust funds and how to play tennis. They took me to country clubs and to eat at places where I couldn't read the menus. Hors d'oeuvres? Entrées? Foie gras? Escargot? Boeuf bourguignon?

The 3.89 GPA I earned at Tech made me a prize among TCU's eight fraternities. Invitations to rush parties showed up in the mail—the tickets to social significance in my new world.

Guy went into all-out recruiting mode for his frat: Sigma Alpha Epsilon. When I walked through the front door and headed to a corner of the lounge, Guy appeared at my side and ushered me in a different direction.

"Don't go over there," he said in a low voice, the same voice that Mom had used to warn me away from the colder water in the Piggly Wiggly.

"Why?"

"That's where they put the geese."

"Geese?"

"Yeah, you know. The squirrely guys, the nerds."

"Uh, oh, thanks."

As he led me away, I took one last look at those poor pimply, unattractive guys on the couch hoping for fraternal heaven. At first, I felt grateful to not be among them. Tomorrow, they would receive a note in their TCU mailboxes informing them that they had been cast into the outer darkness by the fraternal gods of the campus, just like I had been at Texas Tech.

But I couldn't keep away this thought: *Those boys look like some of the kids in my Young Life club.*

My first semester at TCU, a middle-aged, bearded, paunchy Anthropology professor asked, "How many of you believe in eternal life?"

His tone told me he didn't and thought anyone who did was a fool.

Of the thirty-five students in the class, only Guy, a girl across the room, and I raised our hands.

The professor chuckled at our naïveté.

"Have you ever seen a soul?" he said.

The rest of the class let out a courtesy laugh.

If he had really wanted someone to answer his question, I would have pointed out the implications of making what can be seen the ultimate criterion for existence. It would mean the professor had never had a thought, since thoughts can't be seen.

But I guess he hadn't thought about that.

It broke Guy's heart when I picked Phi Delta Theta, in large part for its motto: a Phi is always a gentleman.

But it took one semester to disabuse me of the notion that there could ever be anything gentlemanly about fraternities. For that first semester, I pledged to do anything the brothers at Phi Delta asked. It wasn't so bad until Hell Week—that 168-hour period that exists to empower the sadistic tendencies of boys still confused about the nature of manhood.

At the end of the semester, Hell Week was the only barrier for pledges becoming brothers. And if you had made it that far, you would do just about anything to keep from being cast out among the lost and lonely.

We ate Vaseline sandwiches, chewed raw liver until it turned into liquid in our mouths, and drank an emetic that ranchers used to make cows vomit. We allowed ourselves to be degraded in a host of other ways too revolting to mention in the name of brotherhood.

The next year, I became the assistant pledge trainer to help protect the pledges from some of the worst members. We took our pledges to a ranch at night, where the members cursed them like drill sergeants and made them run around so they could trip them and laugh. But when one of my fellow pledges from the previous year stuck his foot out and tripped a six-foot-six freshman, I could not suppress my rage.

I knew this boy from my Young Life club at Richland High School. His name was Ricky, and he had come to TCU on a four-year basketball scholarship.

I helped Ricky stand up and made sure nothing was broken. Then one of the best basketball players in Texas resumed running around a bonfire in the dirt on a ranch late at night so some mindless member could have the pleasure of tripping a defenseless, superior athlete all over again.

I cornered the perpetrator.

"You idiot!" I yelled right into his face.

"Are you stupid enough to risk breaking the leg of a scholarship athlete? Are you on a mission to get our fraternity kicked off campus forever? If you trip him again, I will kick your butt up around your neck."

I am not a fighter. My last fistfight was in junior high, and I lost. I couldn't and wouldn't have kicked his butt. I was enraged and followed a script Mom had written for me since childhood: when enraged, threaten your target with extinction.

That night, the script worked.

I spent one afternoon each week in a seminar with twelve honors students led by a chemistry professor who had rejected the idea of God. After I raised a number of objections to the theory of evolution, such as gaps in the fossil record and the improbability of nothing creating something, he asked me to come to his office for a visit.

"You are an unusual student," he said. "You don't believe in evolution, but you argue against it on scientific grounds instead of religious grounds."

"That's correct," I said. "What are the odds of a single protein molecule occurring by chance, leaving aside the question of where the material to make the molecule had come from?"

"Not good at all," he said.

Then he explained how it could happen anyway. For the next two minutes, he hurled a host of unfamiliar terms and ideas at me. I had fallen into the trap of talking outside my area of expertise.

"I need to give this some more thought," I conceded. So I abandoned the molecular argument for a moral one. "Can I ask you something else?" I said.

"Sure."

"How do you make your moral decisions?"

"From common sense and my experience of what's helpful to people."

"Would you allow other people to do the same?"

"Of course."

"Suppose your teenage daughter falls in love with me. I don't love her, but I seduce her and then drop her. Can you tell me I was wrong?"

"You would have a very irate father to contend with."

"I didn't ask how you would feel. I asked if there is any logical basis on which you could say my behavior was wrong."

"It's wrong to hurt others."

"But suppose I thought I was helping her. Suppose I thought there was no such thing as love. Suppose I thought humans are simply chemical reactions obeying the laws of physics. The sooner she gives up the idea of love, the more free and authentic her life will be. Can you tell me I'm wrong, that I don't have the right to make that decision?"

"I can't."

"Yet your heart tells you I'm wrong. You've embraced a world-view that your heart can't live with."

I had lifted that line of inquiry out of Lewis's *Mere Christianity*.[2] Everyone acts as if there is an absolute law of right and wrong. Every argument about someone's conduct is based on an appeal to a transcendent "ought." But like the law of gravity, the law of right and wrong does not have a human origin.

The professor then made his concession.

"We should talk again," he said.

We never did.

During my junior year, the gentlemen of Phi Delta Theta threw a bachelor party for one of our brothers and rented a stripper. We pushed our chairs into a huge circle inside a barn.

A thin woman with black hair strolled into the center and undressed to the beat of "In-A-Gadda-Da-Vida."

She tossed her bra to a brother and walked around the circle so everyone could have a closer look. When she came to me, she plopped her butt right down on my lap.

"Oh, honey, you're sitting in the preacher's seat now," a brother yelled. The room erupted in laughter as she performed her routine.

I wasn't prepared for this. I had come to watch, not participate

---

2. C. S. Lewis: *Mere Christianity* (1943; repr., New York: Macmillan, 1960), 17–39.

in, the revelry. Gone was any Christian example I had tried to put forth. I let my hands fall to my sides. I hardened my face into granite to conceal any trace of humiliation.

Finally, she got up and went to another guy, who had a better time with her than I did.

I woke up the next day, feeling not guilty but stupid. Everyone except me knew I did not belong in that barn. God had used a stranger's nakedness to expose me.

In that exposure, I had received a gentle correction, like when Dad took me to the back bedroom. It was too artful to be anything less than divine.

After two years of wasting time, I decided to become independent of Greek society. I made a polite speech to my fraternity brothers that I no longer had the money or the time to be a member (*partly true*), was sorry to leave them (*not at all true*), and would diligently try to hold to the high standard of what they had taught me about always being a gentleman (*you idiots*).

Professor Gustave Ferré wore rumpled coats, outdated ties, and a bright red vest to all his classes, as if the intensity of his intellectual pursuits pushed aside any consideration he might have given to style.

He was fifty-one years old, still slender, six feet tall with sandy hair that was receding and graying. He constantly rubbed his glasses on his red vest while he lectured.

Dr. Ferré was born into a family of overachievers in northern Sweden. His older brother Nils—who had taken his oral PhD exams at Harvard in Latin in front of the great philosopher George Santayana—was a famous theologian. His sister, Thyra Ferré Bjorn, wrote bestselling memoirs about the family.

The brother the family had dubbed its black sheep had become a medical doctor.

Ferré had immigrated to the United States when he was a teenager. He learned to read German, French, Greek, and Hebrew. He took a stab at Sanskrit, he told me in private. He shook his head and said, "Sanskrit defeated me."

During my time at TCU, Ferré was chairman of the philosophy department. He was also a born-again Christian who welcomed challenges to his faith—even when they came from obnoxious students who had just learned from Nietzsche that God is dead.

With a few clever questions, Ferré would expose the weaknesses in their reasoning and kindly undermine the arrogance that caused them to assume their ideas were original.

He could have crushed them. But because of his gentleness, I watched them escape humiliation, saying, "Oh, I see now. Thank you, Dr. Ferré."

I took every class I could from him.

He showed us how philosophers had honed the cosmological argument. If the universe were eternal, "today" would never have arrived because it would still be stretching backward into eternity. An infinite regress is a logical impossibility. Therefore the universe must have had a beginning. A beginning was an event. Events must have a cause, for nothing causes nothing. The Cause had to be both eternal and immaterial since it caused time and space.

Plato called this cause Father.

Ferré gave equal time to the philosophers who denied God's existence, including Friedrich Nietzsche, whose works I read far beyond what was assigned in class.

Nietzsche hated what I found beautiful. I wanted to know why. I expected tightly reasoned assaults on my faith. Instead I sifted through rambling assertions, sometimes semi-poetic, about the freedom of nihilism.

Of all the atheistic philosophers, the French existentialists Jean-Paul Sartre and Albert Camus were my favorite. They understood the consequences of a world devoid of eternal truth and eternal values and seemed to deal with them honestly.

"There is but one truly serious philosophical problem, and that is suicide," read the opening line of Camus' *The Myth of Sisyphus*.[3]

One hundred eighteen pages of lyrical, philosophical prose followed. Camus ended the work with a five-page meditation on Sisyphus, the first king of Corinth in Greek mythology. Sisyphus's cruel, crafty hubris enraged the gods. Zeus condemned him to eternal, bone-weary frustration by forcing him to roll a huge, enchanted boulder up a long, steep hill, only to have it roll back down.

Camus ended the book by asserting that those who had decided against suicide could only find meaning in life by believing a lie.

"One must," he wrote, "imagine Sisyphus happy."[4]

The objections to the Christian faith always came back to one unavoidable aspect of human existence: suffering. God could be either good or omnipotent, but not both. If he were both, how could suffering still exist?

God never answers this question. Instead he suffered.

"My God, my God!" cried Jesus on the cross. "Why have you forsaken me?"

God didn't answer his own Son. He allowed him to be torn apart by the mystery.

Yet Jesus' suffering had redeemed me, and it was so much easier to imagine that my pain would someday be redeemed than to imagine Sisyphus happy.

By the time I was twenty, I knew my real problem was not suffering, but evil. Not how to explain it, but how to refuse it. On this matter, Camus, Sartre, and Nietzsche had nothing helpful to say.

---

3. Albert Camus, *The Myth of Sisyphus and Other Essays* (1955; repr., New York: Vintage, 1991), 3.

4. Camus, *Myth of Sisyphus*, 123.

Nineteen

With Scott's exile in Oklahoma City, the fate of his Richland High Young Life club landed in my inexperienced nineteen-year-old hands. In the fall of 1968, one year ahead of schedule, I stood before 125 high school kids on a Monday night. I tried to follow the same script I had seen from my mentor.

In those days, Young Life relied on a formula that spread out the good news over several messages: *God loves us. Jesus is God. Sin separates us from God. Jesus died on the cross to pay for our sin. Faith makes us right before God.*

But as the evening of my first talk neared, my stomach twisted into a noose that choked out all my confidence. When I rehearsed the talk in front of the mirror in the privacy of my own bathroom, I stammered.

My first time on stage, it took less than a minute for me to recognize boredom in teenage faces that Scott had so easily enthralled. Sweat trickled down my temple. My hands turned clammy.

The message I thought I had memorized got lost in panic. I noticed the expressions in the audience shift from apathy to pity.

Oh no! I thought. *They feel sorry for me!*

The torture ended after about fifteen minutes. I tried to tell more than a hundred teenagers that God loved them. But I had delivered a different message: *If God loved anyone in that room, it wasn't me.*

Separated by hundreds of miles of West Texas prairie, Charlotte and I had agreed we would see other people. A TCU cheerleader and I had become a couple. When the Texas Tech football team came to play TCU, I bumped into Charlotte in the stands at Amon Carter Stadium.

"Hi," I said.

She held her breath for just a second and then let out a nervous laugh. "What are you doing here?" she asked.

"I go to school here now, remember?"

As Charlotte's face turned crimson, my cheerleader girl ran up to me. She ignored the dark-haired beauty dressed in Red Raider red and kissed me on my mouth, marking out her territory. She hugged me and told me she would find me at halftime. Then she skipped down the stadium stairs and joined the other cheerleaders down on the field.

I turned back to Charlotte. I longed for her, not the cheerleader, but I made my face a mask of indifference.

"It was nice to see you," I said. Then I walked away.

But before I took my seat in the stadium, I had planned a trip to Tech.

The next time I stood on the stage at my Young Life club, the crowd had dropped to below one hundred. Then it went to seventy-five, then fifty, then twenty-five.

I hated the weekends because they signaled a countdown to my Monday night humiliation. But time and again, I returned to that stage to confront my weakness.

I tried to meet kids at high school lunches and football games and invite them to Young Life club. But my brain lurched from subject to subject, grasping for common ground with the tenth-grade kid sitting across from me. I could debate the finer points of

John Stuart Mill's empiricism with just about anyone I encountered in academia. But kids just a few years my junior unraveled me.

The encounters became exercises in withstanding rejection. But those exercises didn't make me any stronger.

I cared more about what the kids thought of me than I cared about the kids.

After I bumped into Charlotte at the football game, Guy and I launched the Texas Tech shuttle run. One weekend a month, we would bow our heads, pray for our safety, and point Guy's Grand Sport Buick west on Highway 199. The speedometer seldom drifted below 90.

We crammed a five-hour drive into a four-hour race so I could spend a few precious hours with Charlotte and Guy could hang out with Charlotte's friend Cindy.

We arrived at Tech in a rainstorm. Seventy-five yards of soaked grass separated the street from the entrance to the girls' dorm. We had no umbrellas. Guy didn't hesitate. He popped the front tires over the curb and plowed ruts in the lawn as we passed West Texas boys coming to pick up their dates, forcing some to move out of the way. I thought, *One of those cowboys will put his boot . . .* Instead they looked at us with envy when our girls laughed at our car parked at their front steps.

On the way back to TCU, Guy and I shared a six-pack of beer. I rarely drank in college and never in public. I was supposed to be an example. But when no one else was around, Guy and I felt free to violate minor prohibitions such as speed limits and not drinking before your twenty-first birthday. Both of us were twenty.

The cop pulled us over just outside Olney, Texas, for exceeding ninety miles per hour. The one-room courthouse looked like a set for *Little House on the Prairie*. We could see the jail through a side door.

The judge betrayed no irritation at two city boys for yanking him out of bed in the middle of the night. Guy charmed him. The judge revealed he had a fondness for TCU.

Then the patrolman announced, "The court of such and such district is now in session." The affability vanished from the judge's face.

"The court has charged you with speeding and underage drinking," he said. "How do you want to plead?"

Guy stood up and rested his hands on the tiny table reserved for the defendants.

"Well, you see, your Honor," Guy said, "we are Christians. And we work in a ministry called Young Life that helps wayward high school students who won't go to church because a lot of these kids come from broken homes, and they don't have good role models.

"Some of them get drunk, and some of them use drugs. And we never drink in Fort Worth because we wouldn't want to set a bad example for the kids. But this weekend we were away from the kids and with our girlfriends at Texas Tech, and well, you know, your Honor, we just felt the freedom in Christ to drink a couple of beers, your Honor—"

"Do you believe in the Bible?" the voice behind us boomed.

We turned around, surprised that the patrolman had turned into the prosecutor.

"Yes sir," replied Guy.

"The whole Bible?" asked the patrolman.

"Yes sir," said Guy.

"Then what about Romans 13:1–2?"

Guy looked at me. He makes people laugh; I'm the one who spouts Bible verses. But I didn't know this one. I shrugged.

We were doomed.

"Guilty," said the judge.

Guy handed a $150 check to the Scripture-quoting cop. Guy turned the car east toward civilization, and the first thing I did was look up Romans 13:1–2. I read it aloud to Guy:

> Let everyone be subject to the governing authorities, for there is no authority except that which God has established. The authorities that exist have been established by God. Consequently, whoever rebels against the authority is rebelling against what God has instituted, and those who do so will bring judgment on themselves.

"How did we miss that?" I asked Guy.

Then I spotted the remainder of the six-pack on the floor of the car. The cop forgot to confiscate it.

"I don't know," Guy said.

I handed him a beer.

My life split into two worlds. In one, I implored kids to embrace Jesus and turn away from drunkenness, drugs, and sex. In the other, I was addicted to the exploration of Charlotte's body.

On Monday nights, I spouted the same Christian cliché that was doled out to me: "Lust can't wait to get, but love always waits to give."

But the truth is, love doesn't wait; it endures. I didn't understand the difference.

I kept crossing sexual boundaries. Was I disrespecting her? Did those boundary transgressions mean I didn't love her?

As we spiraled closer toward sex, I underlined a passage in C. S. Lewis's *The Four Loves* about *eros*—the Greek term for romantic love:

> Nothing is shallower than the belief that a love which leads to sin is always qualitatively lower—more animal or more trivial—than one which leads to faithful, fruitful and Christian marriage. The love which leads to cruel and perjured unions, even to suicide-pacts and murder, is not likely

to be wandering lust or idle sentiment. It may well be Eros in all his splendour; heart-breakingly sincere; ready for every sacrifice except renunciation.[1]

I was about as in love as a boy could be. But that love was not a justification for marriage or a guarantee we wouldn't sin. It was all right there in this passage from Lewis, but I couldn't understand it.

———

As the year dragged on, Guy's comic genius enthralled a growing crowd of teenagers on Monday nights at Southwest High School on the opposite side of town.

My crowd dwindled to a handful. The evidence said I should quit. But I wouldn't give up. Scott had never quit on me. And Mom's beatings had taught me how to endure pain and confront fear.

By the end of the school year, I had reduced Scott's club at Richland High to fifteen kids.

We held our last meeting in someone's backyard. Guy stopped by to witness my debacle. He stood in the back, grinned, and shook his head.

We both knew I was a disaster.

———

In the fall of 1969, I was at Tech with Charlotte on my twenty-first birthday. She made me a serape like Clint Eastwood wore in his earlier Westerns—only she made it out of leather, not wool. It weighed too much to be practical. I wore it in Young Life skits and at retreats. It was the most prized garment in my closet.

On Valentine's Day in our junior year, Charlotte gave me an 8 x 10 photograph of herself. She sat on top of a ladder, dressed in a

1. C. S. Lewis, *The Four Loves* (1960; repr., New York: Harcourt, 1991), 108.

red nightshirt, bare legs dangling. She looked through a cardboard cutout of a heart held up in front of her face, to symbolize the gift of her heart to me.

"My girlfriends looked so sexy on the ladder, but I look so silly," she said.

"You look great. You are sexy."

I wanted to tell her, *You're the most beautiful girl in the world. I can't believe you've given me your heart. Please don't ever take it back.*

When we were together, we thought our thoughts and talked our talks, and the sum of it all was "us." We weren't interested in each other's worlds, only in the world of us, the world our love created for us three or four nights each month. We were always face-to-face, never side by side. We shared no purpose in life other than to be together.

Still, neither of us felt secure enough to say what we really wanted to say to the other.

I thought I could protect our love by drawing a line on our bodies. But we crossed that line, and I drew another one. We never fought over sex. Both of us went home wanting more.

Soon only one line remained. I told myself everything would be okay as long as we didn't cross that line. But if we did, our lives would be ruined.

Crossing that boundary would prove our love was not real. And if our love wasn't real, we were meant for another. And we would have maimed the future relationship with our true soul mates.

"Can you two get married?" Charlotte's pastor asked me.

"We want to, but her parents are against it, and she loves her parents and doesn't want to hurt them."

"Why are they against you two marrying?"

"They believe rich girls shouldn't marry poor boys."

"Is that all?"

"Well, my family doesn't have the best history. And I may

become a full-time Young Life leader when I graduate. That's worse than being a pastor in her father's eyes."

"Can you talk to them about marrying their daughter?"

"I don't think so. In five years, I've never had more than a two-sentence conversation with either of them, let alone a meal with them in their home. They don't like me."

His words were devoid of judgment, but he had no solution for us except marriage.

———————

I spent the summer of 1969 in Buena Vista, Colorado, at Young Life's Frontier Ranch. The camp was carved into the side of a mountain and overlooked valleys that turned golden in the sun.

For a week at a time, Frontier Ranch hosted hundreds of kids from all over the country who listened to some of the best speakers I'd ever heard. One used the lyrics of a Rolling Stone song for an illustration. Another invoked the name of Bullet Bob Hayes— then the fastest man alive—when he spoke about Peter and John's race to Jesus' empty tomb. They seldom spoke for more than five minutes without making the crowd laugh. They never yelled. It was like spending thirty minutes with an older best friend who knew you and identified with all your struggles.

It was unlike anything I had heard in church. These speakers didn't condemn the kid's world. They brought God into it. As I listened, I lost all sense of time.

I also took notes.

That fall, eighty kids showed up to the first Young Life Club of the school year. I made them howl with stolen jokes. I turned them somber with plagiarized illustrations. At the end, I promised them I would swallow a live goldfish if they got 125 kids to come to club the next week.

The kids cheered.

The next Monday afternoon, I played touch football with

some guys and rammed my right shoulder into an opponent's chin. At first, I thought the ripping sound was his jaw detaching from its socket. But when I jumped to block a pass on the next play, I couldn't lift my right arm. As my feet hit the ground, I felt nauseating pain compounded by spasms—my right side was on fire. I ran to the sidelines for help.

One of my teammates asked, "Does your shoulder always look like that?"

"Like what?"

"Like that."

When I looked at my right shoulder, it was gone. My collarbone popped up level with my cheek, pushing the skin up like a pup tent. My shoulder blade had slid down my back. And the head of my humerus dangled down where my bicep used to be. In doctor-speak, it was a complete acromioclavicular joint separation.

"Let's get you to the trainer," one of my friends said.

As they opened the door of the car, I passed out. They had to haul me onto the trainer's table. When the TCU trainer cut my jersey off, he called out to the junior trainers.

"Gather around, boys. I want you to see what a complete AC separation looks like."

He pressed my collarbone back into place and then released it so the junior trainers could see it pop up into the air. He said my shoulder was in three pieces now—scapula, clavicle, and humerus—all going their separate ways.

"Son," he said, "I'm gonna tape that arm up so you can't move it, but it's gonna hurt like hell. Ain't nothin' I can do about that. You gotta get to the doc and have him put it back together."

I drove home with my left hand. At 6 p.m., I had a 103-degree temperature. The trainer had not lied. My shoulder hurt like hell. I had no pain medication. The Young Life club started in an hour and a half. My chest and right side were wrapped in Ace bandages and tape. I couldn't take a shower. It took an eternity to change my clothes. On the way to the meeting, the road got blurry.

When I arrived, rowdy kids filled the huge game room of the house where we met. The furniture had been moved to the edges of the room, and the kids were seated on the floor. After the singing, we counted heads—127.

Out came the fish bowl. I picked the goldfish up by his tail. I dangled him over my mouth. The girls squealed. He flapped. Then I put him in my mouth, and everyone screamed. I pulled him out, still flapping. They screamed louder. Finally it went down the hatch. I opened my mouth so everyone could see—no goldfish. Then I gyrated as if I could feel him swimming in my stomach and faked convulsions as if I was about to retch on the front row.

After the applause died, I held the Bible in my left hand and talked to 127 kids about the deity of Jesus Christ and his love for them.

I never saw pity in the eyes of an audience again.

———

Close to the end of our junior year, Charlotte sneaked into Fort Worth to spend the weekend at my house. We hid her car at Mom's boyfriend's used car lot.

We stood at the foot of my bed, lights off, our faces illuminated by moonlight. Then we undressed. We came as close to having sex as we could. After it was over, both of us were quiet for a few moments. I walked her to her bedroom and kissed her good night.

I woke up on Sunday morning with terror a thousand times stronger than the dread that invaded me after the prostitute. I thought I had come within seconds of ruining two young lives.

It didn't occur to me that God might not see much of a difference between crossing a line and dancing on it. It didn't occur to me to talk to him about our struggles. I knew what he wanted: obedience. It didn't occur to me that I might have exchanged the

God who bore the weight of my sin for the God who weighed my sin.

If I spent one more night with her, the damage would be irrevocable. I was like the addict who wakes up in the ICU after an overdose, saddled with the clearest of choices: sobriety or death. God or Charlotte. I could not find a way to love them both.

Later that morning, I took her back to the car lot to her Chevy Impala. I waited until the last possible moment to deliver the blow. I stood beside her as she sat in the driver's seat, ready for the three-hundred-mile trip back to Texas Tech.

She was radiant with love, so beautiful.

I was filled with dread, so resolute.

"We have to break up," I said.

She looked up at me through the car window and laughed, as if it were a joke.

"What?" she said.

"If we see each other again, we'll go all the way," I said.

The color drained from her face. "No, we won't," she pleaded.

"We will. I can't believe we didn't go all the way last night."

"I know we have a problem, but we can fix it. We don't have to break up."

"We do. It's the only way."

Tears rolled down her cheeks.

"Good-bye," I said.

She wept as she put the car in drive. As I watched her car disappear in traffic, I believed I had saved both our lives.

It was one of the cruelest things I have ever done.

Twenty

In high school, my first Bible study was with Bruce, who had led me to God. Our study was on the Sermon on the Mount in Matthew 5–7. In the story, crowds gathered around Jesus, so he walked up a hill to be heard. Then Jesus uttered one statement after another that undermined the foundational principles of the world as he described those who are truly blessed: *the meek and poor in spirit; the merciful, the pure in heart, and the peacemakers; those who are persecuted and reviled for his sake; those who hunger and thirst for righteousness; those who mourn.*

As a seventeen-year-old, I didn't just read those words; I absorbed them. Anything that counterintuitive had to be true.

By my senior year in college, I never watched TV. If I wasn't with high school kids in the evenings, I sat in a black Naugahyde chair in my bedroom and read the Bible, philosophy, and theology. That chair was the place where I surveyed an ocean of truth with an unreachable depth. I sat in it the minute I came home, dragged myself out of it long enough to eat dinner, and stayed in it until I fell asleep.

———

Teddy had joined Guy and me in Young Life. One of the reasons all our clubs grew was the amount of time we spent with kids outside of school activities and outside of the club meetings on Monday night. I took my guys to play handball during the week and on the weekends. Several of the kids had ski boats, so we took kids to water-ski on the weekends. We had weekend retreats at their parents' lake houses.

One weeknight, I went with four of my guys to shoot rats in a big metal barn. The guys had .22 rifles. I had a .22 revolver in a fast draw holster. We started at one end of the pitch-black barn. One guy shined a spotlight at the ceiling, and the rats ran for cover while we shot at them. Then we turned the light off, waited for a few minutes, walked a few more steps, shined the light on the roof, and commenced shooting again. We worked our way to the far end of the barn, and one of the guys shot a fat monster. The rat plopped behind a sack of grain. The shooter ran to claim his trophy. I walked off to the side of the guys, slipped my revolver out of the holster, and pointed it at the ground away from the guys. The shooter held up the giant rat by his tail in the glare of the spotlight. I said, "I'm going to shoot that rat right out of your hand," and I fired my gun into the ground. The guy, Ricky, screamed and threw the rat into the air and began instinctively rubbing his left hand. Everyone laughed.

By the fall of 1970, my Young Life club swelled to 250 kids. The high school principal gave me unfettered access to the campus. The nurse allowed me to use her office for private meetings. As my senior year began, one of the most popular girls in the junior class needed to talk.

"I don't know what to do," she said. "I've ruined my life. I can't tell my parents. It would break their hearts."

Her boyfriend had pledged her his eternal love, and she had given him her virginity. But his eternal love ran out three weeks after she gave in.

"No one will want to marry me now—not anyone I would want to marry. I thought he was the one. I thought he loved me," she said.

"You made a mistake, but your life is not over. You are not damaged goods. God will forgive you in a heartbeat," I told her.

"Really?"

"Absolutely."

"Do you think God will bring him back to me?"

"I don't know. But you deserve better."

"How can you say that?"

"Because God loves you, and he has a wonderful guy for you. A guy who won't love you because of what you've done or not done. A guy who will love you for who you are."

"Really?" her face brightened.

"For sure," I promised.

I believed that this girl hadn't ruined her life, though I maintained that Charlotte and I would have ruined ours. This girl's boyfriend had been heartless, but me? I had been protecting both of us.

In my Young Life community, people saw me as a paragon of purity and theological knowledge. In my heart of hearts, I did not disagree.

Although I loved the poetry of Jesus' Sermon on the Mount, I remained oblivious to its truth. People who already feel righteous don't hunger and thirst for it.

After the conversation with the junior who had been swindled out of her virginity, I put out the word that I planned to give a sex talk for the girls on Thursday afternoon next week.

The girls filled the huge den. All the furniture had been moved out or shoved to the walls. I told them how I first learned about sex after the beating my mother gave me for saying the f-word in the kitchen.

A day after the lashing, I asked my third-grade friend Dennis, whose mother was a nurse, what the f-word meant, and he provided the grossest explanation of sex.

"I will never do that," I vowed in disgust.

"That's not the worst part," Dennis said. "That's how babies are made."

Then I thought about my parents.

I thought I knew them. Those perverts. Maybe I'll go live with Nonnie. But wait a minute . . . She made Mom and Uncle Ralph Jr. How far back does this perversion go in our family line?

Then Dennis dropped a morsel of relief.

"That's not the only way to get babies," he said.

"It's not?" I asked.

"You can also go to the hospital to get them," he said.

Thank goodness. I, my brothers, and my sister were all born in Harris Methodist Hospital.

That story was my icebreaker. Then I asked how many of them had had a talk about sex with their parents. A few raised their hand.

I explained the difference in the biology of arousal for men and women. I told them that everything started with the kiss, and that kisses were subject to the law of diminishing returns, and that desire would erase every line we drew on our bodies. I told them some of the techniques guys used to make girls go farther than they wanted to. I told them that when guys try to force them to give more than the girls wanted to give, the guys weren't loving them; they were lusting after them. I told them that the guys referred to girls as "a piece" in the locker room because guys did not want them, only a piece of them. My cardinal rule was that "lust can't wait to get, but love always waits to give."

I didn't threaten the kids with God's judgment if they were sexually impure. I told them that God forgives all of our sins and can heal the damage of our worst sins. The main motivation I offered them was positive. God gave us a great gift in sex.

I told them that God had made a wonderful person for each of us who would perfectly complement us. I told them that the question was not about finding that person, but about being the kind of person who would attract the partner of our destiny. Wait for that person and enjoy a lifelong journey of passion, intimacy, and self-fulfillment. I preached the movies to those kids, a life on cruise control that no one ever lives, but it was the life I hoped for.

Before I knew it, I became Young Life's local "sexpert." Parents asked to sit in on the talks I gave at various clubs around town. They didn't know how to discuss sex with their children and wanted to learn from me, a twenty-one-year-old, years away from having his first child. I tried to discourage parents' presence, fearing it would inhibit the dialogue. When I gave one of those sex talks at the home of Bobby Brown, the former Hall of Fame second baseman for the New York Yankees, Brown's wife, Sara, asked to attend.

"Okay," I said, "but you have to sit in the back, and you can't say a word."

Some of the guys complained that because of those talks, the girls weren't so easy anymore. So I invited the guys to a "guys only" sex talk. And they filled up the room, just like the girls had. I became the guy who gave the sex talks at the summer camps of Young Life.

I never told the kids where they should draw the line in relationships. I told them where I drew mine. I would not kiss a girl again until I met the girl I would marry. Everything started with The Kiss. If I didn't kiss the girl, I would never have sex with the girl. My next kiss would mean, *I love you and want to marry you.*

My next kiss would be the greatest kiss in the world. It would launch us into a never-ending euphoria.

A year had passed since I ended things with Charlotte. Graduation approached, and I still wondered if she was the one. So I called her on her birthday—not to say happy birthday, but to see if she was my forever girl.

"Hello," she answered.

"Hi, how are you?" I asked.

I heard her catch her breath as she had at the football game years earlier, and then nervous laughter.

"I didn't expect to hear from you again," she said.

"I think we should see each other again," I said.

"So do I."

I stood in front of her door on a late afternoon in May when her parents were away. When she opened the door, she looked as beautiful as ever. But the magic was missing.

We went to the movies. We swam in her pool. As we sat on her deck, drying out in the sun, I asked her if she planned to get a master's degree in Art.

"I don't know," she said. "I'm not sure what I want to do. Do you realize this is the first time you've ever asked about my plans for my life?"

The conversation lulled, and we both stared out over the pool.

"I'm getting married," she said.

Her words hit harder than any punch. I felt so stupid. I had assumed in the absence of "us" that she had lived a celibate life like me.

"Is he a Christian?" I asked.

"Oh, yes," she said. My gut said she lied or was deceived.

"He's predictable. I feel secure with him. With you, I never know where I stand," she said.

So much for my keep-her-guessing strategy.

"And we come from similar economic backgrounds," she said.

The low blow stunned me. What did money have to do with love?

I followed her into her house, unable to believe this was really good-bye. When I hugged her, her arms stayed limp at her sides. I wanted to kiss her. I wanted to say, "I love you. Come away with me." But it didn't feel right. Then my arms went limp.

"Good-bye," I said.

"Good-bye."

I drove home, collapsed in my bed, cried, and wondered if I had just made the greatest mistake of my life. In my grief, I realized how she must have felt when I watched her drive off into the desert after I abruptly severed ties.

I told God I was sorry for how I treated her. I told him I was sorry I had failed him and her in our physical relationship. A familiar presence invaded the darkness of my bedroom, and I was at peace again.

I had thought my last visit was for me to figure out if she was my forever girl. But God had used my ego and thoughtlessness to give her a wedding gift far better than anything on her registry. For her, that last visit was proof that the world of "us" no longer existed.

Now she could walk down the aisle free of the boy who could never say what he really felt, who had tried to hold on to her with feigned indifference, and who was never interested enough to ask her about her future.

———

The wedding announcement appeared in the *Fort Worth Star-Telegram* in the fall.

"Are you going?" Bruce asked.

"I didn't get an invitation."

"She would want you to come."

I hoped not.

Twenty-One

Teddy, Guy, and I resented Scott's replacement, Dale, our new Young Life boss, but only because he wasn't Scott.

Scott was funny; Dale was serious. Scott was in his twenties; Dale was in his thirties. Scott was single; Dale was married with children.

We called him "Dull" behind his back.

The only thing "Dull" had in common with Scott was that he had also been a college wrestler. I assumed that the vigor of youth outweighed age and experience. I wrestled him once. It took a month to get the full use of my left shoulder back. I never called him Dull again.

Dale's knowledge of Scripture surpassed his repertoire of wrestling moves. When I told Dale I didn't understand an obscure passage that referenced a seventy-week period somewhere in the Old Testament, he knew exactly where it was.

"Oh, you mean Daniel 9:24–27," Dale replied.

He explained why he believed the passage described various events at the end of the world. Later, when I inquired about the possibility of errors in Scripture, Dale rattled off six passages proving that God breathed out the Bible. Dale explained that these verses did not prove the Bible was inerrant, but they did prove that the biblical writers, as well as Jesus, all believed the Bible had no errors. And if we could trust Jesus to take us to heaven, surely we could trust him to teach us the truth about the Bible. When I asked

Dale if a believer could lose eternal life, he listed all the passages that indicated salvation was a gift that couldn't be taken back, a gift that couldn't even be given back. Then he detailed verses that seemed to conflict with that doctrine and showed me how they had been misinterpreted.

Now I felt as helpless as I had when he pinned me to the floor.

"Where did you learn all this?" I asked.

"It was required in seminary," he said.

He didn't just attend any seminary; Dale graduated from Dallas Theological Seminary—a fortress of theological fundamentalism. Now I knew what I wanted to do after TCU. In the fall of 1970, I applied to Dallas Seminary. Guy and Teddy joined me.

At DTS, students took classes on every book in the Bible in their four years of study, and they also had four years of systematic theology. But the most difficult part of the education was the required eight semesters of New Testament Greek and five semesters of Old Testament Hebrew. No exceptions. No substitutions.

Many students groaned about hours spent on languages no longer spoken, languages they would never use once they graduated to their real lives. Not me. The syntax of participles and infinitives, of genitives and accusatives, made me happy. I sat quietly in the back of irrelevant classes, tuned out the professor who said nothing I could not read more quickly in books, and redeemed the boring hours by writing out the entire Greek and Hebrew paradigms for the strong and weak verb. Within a year, I had the Greek and Hebrew verbal systems down cold. Then I added Aramaic to my exegetical arsenal.

I majored in three professors. S. Lewis Johnson Jr. and Zane Hodges were incredible New Testament exegetes and superb preachers. And then there was Bruce Waltke, Dallas Seminary's beautiful mind. They were my three icons.

Waltke wore glasses and had a high forehead with a little

squiggle of hair dangling down. He loved to toss around Latin phrases, like *lectio difficilior*, in his high-pitched voice. More myths than the Greek pantheon followed him through the hallowed halls of Dallas Seminary.

A student told me that in a final exam at Harvard, Waltke wrote a quote in Latin and then, unaware, finished the exam in Latin. Another said he quoted a German source during a lecture and spoke in German until a student stopped him. And still another said Dr. Waltke had made the highest grades in the history of Harvard.

"That is not true," he said when I asked him about it.

———

At the end of my first semester, Mom found the money for me to go on a ten-day tour of Israel over Christmas break, led by Dr. Waltke.

On that ten-day trip in Israel, I jostled close to the front of the tour. I had never witnessed anything like the encyclopedic knowledge that flowed out of Waltke as we traversed the basalt ruins of Capernaum, the windswept mesa of Masada, and the marlstone cliffs at the Qumran caves.

That spring, I added Waltke's Old Testament Archaeology class to my already full schedule. It was considered the most difficult class in the seminary. Seniors and even some professors populated the course. When Waltke handed out the final exam, the student next to me went catatonic.

"God couldn't pass this exam," he said.

A week later, our graded tests appeared in our seminary mailboxes. On the first page of my blue book exam was a personal note from Dr. Waltke: *Highest grade in the class.*

I enrolled in every course he offered.

In his class on the Hebrew text of the psalms, Waltke had us study Psalm 139:17–18, which is traditionally translated (emphasis added):

How precious *to me* are your thoughts, God!
How vast is the sum of them!
Were I to count them,
they would outnumber the grains of sand.

Part of our assignment was to find the meaning of the preposition *to* in the first line. In English, the word *to* can be used in at least twenty ways, and these can be summarized in a single paragraph. But the standard Hebrew lexicon devoted eight-and-a-half large, double-columned, fine-print pages to the preposition *to*. There are hundreds of ways to use it.

After I spent hours reading through all the relevant examples in the lexicon, I was sure that the traditional translation "to me" in verse 17 had to be wrong.

The verse should be translated (emphasis added):

How precious are your thoughts *about me*, God!
How vast is the sum of them!
Were I to count them,
they would outnumber the grains of sand.

A preposition changed the entire meaning of these two verses. God's thoughts *about* me outnumbered the grains of the earth's sand—even when he was far from my mind. Studying the various uses of *to* had unlocked another realm of profundity about God's boundless love for me. But I was more enthralled with my increasing ability to extract truth from the Scripture rather than the truth itself.

———

In one of my first classes, a professor said to us, "Liberals feel; we think." The students roared. The message was clear. *Feelings are your enemy. They cloud your mind and endanger your faith.*

I embraced that message. Seminary erected barriers that kept me from processing the trauma of my youth, and some of this was a blessing. But left untreated, wounds fester.

Friendship was the highest value in my Young Life community. I trained my college friends to become friends with high school students so they could help those students begin a relationship with God.

At Dallas Seminary, the highest value was knowing the Bible and believing in the seminary's interpretation of the Bible.

It's safe to say that not one faculty member at Dallas would have ever denied that a historical Jesus walked up a mountain two thousand years earlier to deliver the sermon about the blessed.

But when they stood on their own mounts, some of them rewrote the Beatitudes on the hearts of their students.

They traded *blessed are the meek* for *blessed are the learned*, and *blessed are the poor in spirit* for *blessed are the pure in doctrine*.

Twenty-Two

For my first two years of seminary, I didn't go on a single date because I couldn't find anyone who compared to Charlotte. I wondered if I was destined for celibacy, like one of those medieval theologians.

Then on May 18, 1973, I saw her get out of the backseat of a yellow Pontiac coupe in the noonday heat.

And I thought, *What idiot put her in the backseat?*

The possibility of my celibacy evaporated in the East Texas heat.

This petite girl was the softest, most sensual beauty I had ever seen.

She had long dark brown hair, soft and glistening in the sunlight. I had only seen that kind of hair in shampoo commercials. I imagined what it would be like to put my hands in her hair and pull her to me. I could no more put her beauty into words than an explanation of Beethoven's Ninth Symphony could capture its magical power. You had to hear the music. You had to see her.

The insecure boy who was paralyzed at the sight of a beautiful fourteen-year-old girl a decade earlier in the lobby of the Hollywood Theatre had vanished. In his place was Young Life's revered sexpert and the seminary's boy wonder who, at twenty-four, thought of himself as an authority on purity, love, and romance.

I walked right up to her.

"How was your flight?" I asked.

"Fine," she said. "It's my first time in Texas."

Her name was Leesa. She was nineteen years old, and she was from Scottsdale, Arizona.

I had come to East Texas for the summer of 1973 because some businessmen who served on the Young Life committee offered me an insane amount of money—$800 a month—to oversee a summer work crew of twenty-five Young Life college kids. They thought these bright and beautiful college kids working at the resort community, Holly Lake, would sell more lake property.

I looked for Leesa after lunch, but she had disappeared. She was absent that whole afternoon. I asked her friend where she was, and the friend confided that Leesa had severe cramps. She hid her pain behind a facade of serenity and grace. I had no clue that she was hurting.

Someone else had to tell me about her pain.

Later that afternoon, Leesa's former Young Life leader who had moved to Texas to become the social director for the resort told me that Leesa had quit a good job as a dental assistant in Scottsdale. Leesa thought a summer spent studying the Scriptures with all the other Young Life kids would draw her closer to the Lord. The resort offered no benefits and paid half what her job in Scottsdale paid.

The next day, I paid Leesa an "official" visit to see how she had settled into her job as a waitress at the resort's restaurant. We sat at a table during her break. I told Leesa how I came to Christ on December 18, 1965. I asked her when she became a Christian, but she could not tell me. She didn't remember a time when didn't know God. She said, "When I was a little girl, I used to go outside at night and look up at the stars and talk to God."

Leesa's Young Life leader said that Leesa had given talks in her Young Life club while she was in high school and that she had become a leader in the same club after she graduated.

I waited a few days and asked her if she would like to play

tennis with a couple who were ten years older than me. From that tennis date on, we were a couple. We saw each other every day. Lunches, dinners, walks, afternoon coffees, and boats on the lake.

One June afternoon, I found Leesa in a lounge chair by the pool. I pulled up a chair beside her and saw a Bible under her chair.

"I don't think I've ever seen anyone bring their Bible to a public pool," I said.

"I do it all the time," she said. "I love to meditate on Scripture while I sit in the sun. It's so calming."

"What are you meditating on today?" I asked.

"Psalm 103. It's one of my favorites."

"What do you like about Psalm 103?"

She opened her Bible to Psalm 103 and read verse 4: "who redeems your life from the pit and crowns you with love and compassion."

"Don't you love that verse?" she asked.

"Yes, I do. It's beautiful," I said.

I was so impressed with her attachment to her Bible that I forgot to ask her why she loved this verse. I could see that God had crowned her with love and compassion, but I was sure she had never been in a pit.

That first week or two, I tried to keep her guessing how I felt about her, but my costume of nonchalance no longer fit—not around her.

As we walked by the lake at night, I casually mentioned a few girls from past Young Life camps who had extended invitations for me to visit them in various cities throughout the country.

She told me about a boat driver at a Young Life camp in Canada who had sent her letters, but then she went quiet.

"What's the matter?" I asked.

"I don't like this game," she said. "I don't see why when you like someone, you have to hide it."

The three guys from Scottsdale who had accompanied her to

Holly Lake told me that Leesa was the most beautiful and beloved girl in her high school. It was not uncommon to see her help a deaf student with her assignments. She had led her boyfriend, the quarterback of the football team, to the Lord. They said she had been the homecoming queen runner-up.

When Leesa told me about her high school life, she offered a different perspective. She and her boyfriend broke up at the end of their senior year. And she still felt the humiliation of being only the runner-up to the homecoming queen.

There was something not quite right, but I couldn't define it. Her serenity was not as perfect as I had first imagined. Leesa was quiet in our group meetings where I taught the Bible and answered questions. She never spoke up or asked a question.

I told her about Dad's suicide and how I used to steal all my clothes.

She said her parents had laughed when she said she wanted to go to college. She wasn't smart enough, they said. They insisted she needed to get married soon, and as added incentive, they kicked Leesa out of the house at eighteen.

She told me about how her father had caught her making out on the couch with her boyfriend in the ninth grade. He beat her bare legs with his belt. In gymnastics, her teacher asked her how her calves had gotten so bruised. She said she had fallen down the stairs. If her teacher wondered how the stairs could create a crisscross pattern of bruises about the width of a man's belt, she didn't ask. It could have been dangerous.

Leesa's father was the mercurial football coach at another high school.

Turns out she had been in a pit.

———————

One evening at the end of June, I drove alone through the lake development on those oil and sand roads that were all over rural

East Texas. I caught myself saying out loud, over and over, "Leesa, Leesa, Leesa . . ." I don't know how long I had been repeating her name or what brought me out of that hypnotic trance.

From the moment I saw Leesa six weeks earlier, my mind had warned me to go slow. *Love at first sight is impossible. You don't really know her yet.* These were the warnings that my mind hurled at my feelings. And yet her name had become a song inside my soul. That had never happened to me before.

Had I found my forever girl, or better, had God brought my forever girl to me? I had not kissed Leesa or even held her hand. I needed a little more certainty before I placed my hand and my future happiness in her hand.

I had reduced Charlotte to an illustration in my sex talks about what not to do in a relationship, but I would still compare Leesa to her. I took a day off in the middle of the week to drive home. In my bedroom, I pulled out the bottom drawer of my desk where I had hidden the 8 x 10 photograph of Charlotte. As I gazed at it, I was grateful for the concrete shoes that had held me in place the last time I saw Charlotte.

I pulled the Clint Eastwood serape out of my closet and found other romantic memorabilia and put it in a pile. Then I carried it all to the trash.

That night, I stood with Leesa alone by the lake under a full moon. I held her hand for the first time. Then I put my arms around her and gave her The Kiss that my purity had saved for three years.

I opened my mouth slightly and gently touched her lips for only a second. Then again with a little more pressure. The Kiss said, "I love you," to the sweetest person I had ever known. I put my left hand in her soft brown hair, the thing I had wanted to do the moment I saw her. I drew her face to my chest. She placed her right hand over my heart. My right arm held her waist.

Leesa did not know that this kiss was my wordless proposal.
We swayed in the moonlight.
"You are so beautiful, kind, and good," I said.
"I'm not good," she said back.
I thought, *Silly girl.*

Twenty-Three

For years, I told students when you love someone enough to marry them, tell them your most shameful secrets. Hold nothing back except the details. If they can't deal with your secrets, let them find out now and leave.

We had the talk in the front seat of a 1969 red Cadillac Coupe DeVille late at night. I told Leesa about the prostitute in Mexico, about my nearly having sex in college, and about being in love with Charlotte for five years.

Then it was her turn. She had loved her high school boyfriend. They had done everything short of intercourse. She looked down when she made her confession.

I told her everything was fine.

My dream of a perfect wedding night was closer than ever. We both had saved the most important thing.

Two days later, Leesa's conscience won out. We were in the front seat of the red Cadillac when she told me she had lied. She had had sex.

So that's what "I'm not good" meant.

Leesa hung her head and stared at the floorboard, as though she could be picked up for a bargain-basement price.

I made sure my face registered no shock, only understanding and acceptance. Once again, I told her everything was okay. She looked relieved. I took her home.

Then I walked into my mobile home and rammed my fist into my black metal filing cabinet.

For the first time ever, I screamed at God. *Is this the thanks I get for saving The Kiss?*

I acted out my tenth Christmas all over again. I still thought I knew better than my Father.

A long time ago, The Kiss had gone from fantasy to expectation. But in real life, couples ride off into storms, not sunsets. The movies bypassed my defenses with good stories and stamped my heart with unhealthy beliefs.

"Love your wives, just as Christ loved the church," the apostle Paul told the Ephesians (5:25). I read that verse hundreds of times, but its meaning eluded me.

Christ had looked at a bride blemished beyond belief and loved her enough to die an infinite death.

But I didn't just want a spotless bride; I thought I deserved one.

I put my hope in The Kiss and turned my future wife into a character. In my movie, she had a role to play. She was a reward to be earned, not a person to be loved. A chasm lies between those two perspectives.

I fell into that chasm, searching for Leesa's wonderful guy, the guy who couldn't be pained by his beloved's sexual past, the guy I promised to all those high school and college girls. I searched everywhere, but all I could find was a big talker with a little heart, a religious boy, a hypocrite who slugged file cabinets and shouted at God and felt things he should not be feeling. I hated that guy. I would not wish him on any girl.

Shouting at God for what?

I tried to answer that single question and created a jet stream of questions in my head. It twisted, turned, split, and flowed in different directions.

As the year wore on, Leesa and I followed the same progression that Charlotte and I had. Only with Leesa, I was unable to stop.

I told God I was sorry, but I did not ask him any questions. He had made it clear in his book that I should wait until after I said, "I do," and the minister stood behind us. So what more was there to talk about?

I had no idea how to find my way back to God. Even my confessions felt fake. If I were truly sorry, I wouldn't sin the same sin over and over. I questioned whether I loved God. I questioned whether I loved Leesa. I questioned whether I loved anyone.

I had no one to help me wash off the guilt and shame that dirtied my soul.

All my heroes were professors now. During the first semester of seminary, I learned that I could not talk to professors about my real life, only about a sanitized version of my religious life.

Two of my friends and I took a professor to lunch. He and I stood outside the car, and I told him how I almost had sex with my college girlfriend, but God had intervened to protect us. I wanted to tell him more, but I saw the pained expression on his face. As soon as I paused, he changed the subject. I thought, *Note to self: Jackie, this is not an acceptable conversation around here. Keep your secrets to yourself.*

I followed that rule as long as I lived in that community.

Every time I heard a pastor talk about their wedding night, they proclaimed gratitude that they arrived with their virginity intact. It was unthinkable for any Christian leader to stand before a congregation and confess that they had followed the path of David and Bathsheba.

So I took my sin underground and suffered in the dark silence.

I no longer knew who I was, but I knew what I was.

Twenty-Four

The day after our wedding, we cruised through the mountains of southern Colorado in the1969 red Coupe DeVille Mom had given us as a wedding gift. My bride stared out the window at snowcapped peaks and sighed.

"I thought you said I would be happy," Leesa said.

"You will," I said. "Just give it some time."

Her sadness was a mystery to me.

My belief in the irrevocable damage of my sin had stolen much of the joy of our courtship and all of my joy in our wedding. To me, our wedding was not a celebration of our love; it was an empty formality to make our sex legal.

All her life, Leesa had imagined her groom telling her how beautiful she was on her wedding night. I was so preoccupied with what I shouldn't have done that I neglected to do what she needed most. When the morning came, Leesa thought I had settled for her out of obligation caused by my sin.

What's worse: sex before marriage, or forgetting to tell the bride how beautiful she is on her wedding night?

After we made it to our mountain cabin hidden in the pines, we made love in front of the roaring fire downstairs. The most intoxicating experience of my life began to melt away my guilt. Leesa's sadness retreated in front of that fire.

When we returned to Fort Worth, we moved into a government-subsidized apartment in Haltom City, a small, poor municipality a few miles northeast of Fort Worth. The couple in the apartment below us woke us often at 3 a.m. with screams of profanity, accusations of infidelity, and threats of bodily harm. Sometimes we heard thuds against the wall.

Every Friday night, we ate with friends at McDonald's or El Chico, which had an enchilada dinner for $1.99. Then we watched a movie at the dollar cinema.

Leesa knew how much I loved food and bought her first cookbook and a Crock-Pot. After I came home from class, Leesa whirled around our tiny kitchen, brown hair fallen over one eye, flour on her cheek, flour on her red-checked apron, flour on the countertop, flour on the floor. Every cabinet door and drawer slung open; measuring cups and spoons were scattered over the counter.

I thought she was the cutest person in the world.

———

Marriage freed me from the guilt of addictive sex outside marriage and lifted me into a realm of peace and sharpened focus. In Dr. Waltke's Contemporary Old Testament Theology class, he quoted from my master's thesis, "Metaphor in the Song of Solomon."

"I'm learning a lot from Jackie Deere's thesis," he said.

The class overflowed with fourth-year students and faculty members, and they all turned to see just who it was that Waltke had so highly praised. Those glances showered me with validation, but I tried to appear as if I didn't need the validation at all.

———

My paradigm of a promiscuity-ruined life continued to crumble.

Leesa worked forty hours a week as a dental assistant. I went to seminary and trained college students to be Young Life leaders.

We didn't have a TV—we wanted to spend our evenings getting to know one another or reading. Leesa curled up next to me on the bed as I read the *Chronicles of Narnia* to her. I loved watching the wonder on Leesa's face. Then I read her Tolkien's *Lord of the Rings*, but the story took her prisoner, and she had to have her own copy.

Leesa turned twenty-one that fall. I took her to the finest restaurant in Fort Worth, the Carriage House. It was a pleasant twenty-first birthday—until dessert came. Then Leesa went dark. She stopped laughing at my jokes. We drove home in silence.

I had spent three months of enchilada money for Leesa's birthday dinner, and I wanted to know where I went wrong.

In the bedroom I asked, "What's the matter?"

"Nothing."

"What are you unhappy about?"

"Nothing. I'm just tired."

"We are not going to sleep until you tell me what's wrong."

"Okay, I'll tell you. Why did you have to look at those pictures?"

"What pictures?"

"You know what pictures."

"I don't have a clue what you are talking about."

"Those nude pictures on the wall at the restaurant."

"What nude pictures?"

"The women with the big breasts."

"What do you mean?"

She meant the wallpaper in the dim, candlelit dining room where we ate. I had been nearsighted since college. I wore glasses to drive, but took them off as soon as I slid out of the car.

"Honey, I didn't even see the wall. I wasn't wearing my glasses."

When Leesa was growing up, her mother and father would not speak to each other after a fight. Leesa sat through weeks of wordless dinners and passive spite. When she disappointed them, they turned their silent rage on her, refusing to say anything to her or even to look at her on the way to school.

Leesa and I had agreed to end these patterns. We had pledged to always talk and never hold on to our anger and sadness.

That night, we talked for an hour and broke a curse that one generation had saddled on the next.

Then we fell asleep in each other's arms.

———

As the spring of 1975 ran out, I lingered after one of Dr. Waltke's classes until we were alone.

"What will you do after graduation, Jackie?" he asked.

"I want to do the doctoral program with you."

"Great! We're going to have so much fun," he said as he hugged me.

My first hug ever from a seminary professor.

In the fall of 1975, Waltke created a new doctoral program in Old Testament Studies for ten students and tossed us into a sea of Hebrew manuscripts and Semitic languages. Every week we wrote papers and then listened to Waltke shred them. I loved it all.

In the middle of the fall semester, Waltke summoned me to his office. He asked how I enjoyed the doctoral program. I told him his lectures and seminars were great. He asked me why I skipped another professor's classes.

"His class isn't necessary," I said. "He doesn't say anything I can't read faster in books."

"But you're the only one skipping his class," Waltke said. "We need to keep the peace around here. I told him I would talk to you like a Dutch uncle."

"It's not the best use of my time, but I'll go to the class just to please you."

The next spring, Waltke announced in class that he was leaving Dallas Seminary. I took a deep breath to harden myself against a grief that had become too familiar. *Not again*, I thought. First Dad, then Scott, and now the most gifted scholar I would ever know.

Why did God take away everyone I looked up to?

I had entered the doctoral program because of Waltke and no one else, and I had made that clear to him more than once. I had intended to write a definitive work on the Song of Solomon under the supervision of one of the greatest Old Testament scholars in the conservative evangelical world. I didn't care about a degree; I cared about knowledge.

With Waltke leaving, I decided to quit the program.

But before I told Waltke I was leaving, he called me into his office again.

"Would you like to teach Hebrew next year?" he asked.

"Yes," I said.

"How many classes would you like to teach?"

"As many as you'll let me."

"Do you want to teach a full load of first-year Hebrew grammar classes?"

"That would be great."

"Okay. I'm appointing you to the Old Testament faculty full-time for two years. There may be something here for you after that. There may not be."

"Thank you very much, Dr. Waltke."

"I'm not sure I'm doing you a favor, Jackie. I'm worried about slowing down your doctoral program."

"Well, I don't think you have to worry about that. The doctoral program will be about 75 percent easier if you leave. So I'll have extra time on my hands for a job."

"It's all settled then."

Twenty-Five

As my star rose, Leesa felt more like a comet that had flared over Scottsdale's horizon and crashed into the mud of Fort Worth. She had been beloved in high school and in the Young Life community of her hometown. In my Young Life circle, everyone had a college degree or worked toward one. But Leesa knew she would never earn a degree. She tried to tell me how unhappy she was, but I couldn't hear her.

I tossed around Hebrew and Greek terms in my talks to the Young Life leaders. She endured those meetings with a serenity that masked her shame.

For the Christmas of 1974, my brother Gary gave me a .22 revolver. I stuck it in a closet and forgot about it. Leesa found the revolver and kept it under the front seat of her car. If nothing got better, she had a way out.

Then she found her lifeline. In December 1975, Leesa walked through our front door with a mischievous smile. She stared at me for a few seconds and then shouted, "I'm pregnant!" and jumped into my arms.

But she started bleeding the next day. I rushed her to the doctor. Her gynecologist, Jim, was a friend of ours, and he had served on the Young Life committee. We had gone skiing together at winter camps with him and his wife.

"Jackie, I don't think Leesa will carry this baby to term," Jim said. "I'll give her some medicine. She should stay in bed. But don't get your hopes up. You both are young, and you'll be able to have other children."

That afternoon, as we cried together on our small green and yellow couch, I did get my hopes up. What if Jim was wrong? I didn't rely on one opinion in theology. Why should I with medicine? My best friend, Craig, had an older brother, Joe, who was a brilliant doctor. I called him.

"What are her symptoms?" he asked.

I told him.

"She has been diagnosed correctly," he said. "There is an 80 percent chance she won't have that baby. And Jackie, if she has that baby, you will spend the rest of your life and most of your finances caring for it. Losing it may be a blessing in disguise."

I took comfort in his words. I expected Leesa would too, but when I told her what Joe had said, she continued crying. Maybe she hadn't heard me. So I repeated it.

Still no response.

I put my hands on her shoulders and turned her toward me in order to make her listen. She broke away.

"I heard you the first time," she said. "I don't care how this baby is born. I want this baby with all my heart. I will take this baby however God gives me my child. I will spend the rest of my life caring for my baby. The worst thing in the world would be to lose this little one."

She continued to weep. I sat there, a silent spectator, unable to comfort, unable to pray. The God I believed in did miracles once, but no longer. How could I pray for what I did not believe in?

I struggled to process Leesa's emotions. She had only learned she was carrying a baby twenty-four hours ago. That baby had made her sick, threatened her ability to have other children, and could even kill her. Yet her love for whatever life remained inside her was so strong that she would gamble away the quality of her future.

RAHAMIM!

The Hebrew term for "womb" exploded in my brain. It can also mean "compassion." A Hebrew husband could not identify with his wife's love for her unborn child, a love so great that she would die for that child. This is how "womb" also became the ancient Israelites' primary word to describe God's compassion for his helpless children trapped in the womb of earthly life. My reason could not penetrate what Leesa felt, because what she felt transcended reason.

She was twenty-two years old, and in the grade school where she worked as a teacher's aide, older teachers who'd had miscarriages tried to offer comfort. "It will be okay," they said. "You'll be able to have other children." Leesa thanked them, but ignored their advice. She wanted *this* child.

She kept praying. Then the bleeding stopped. Leesa thanked God, believing he had healed her. But at sixteen weeks, our doctor could not find the heartbeat with his stethoscope.

"Leesa, I'm sorry," Jim said. "It looks like we'll have to do a D&C."

"No," she said.

"Leesa, the baby's heart is not beating. If we don't do a D&C, you might not be able to have children in the future."

"I can't," she said. "I just can't."

"Okay. We'll wait one more week, but if I don't hear the heartbeat next Friday morning, you have to have a D&C on that day."

Over the next seven days, Leesa besieged heaven.

The next Friday morning, Jim leaned over her abdomen and put a cold stethoscope on her belly.

Nothing.

Tears fell down her cheeks. *Please God, please God, please God, oh please God . . .*

He moved the stethoscope.

Nothing.

O God, please. Please God, please God . . .

One more try. Again, the doctor inched the stethoscope across her belly.

He looked up.

"It's not very strong," he said, "but your baby's heart is beating."

Thank you, God. Thank you! Thank you! Thank you!

Five months later, I stood beside Leesa's bed in Harris Methodist Hospital, south of downtown Fort Worth. I held her hand as she moaned.

"It hurts so much," she gasped.

She had refused the epidural anesthesia because she thought natural childbirth would give our baby a better shot at a healthy birth. After eight hours of induced labor, she was exhausted, soaked in sweat.

At eight o'clock in the evening, on June 28, 1976, I watched Stephen Craig Deere emerge from Leesa's womb. Perfect and healthy.

Leesa laughed and cried as the nurses washed the blood off Stephen and placed him in his mother's arms. Drained and disheveled, Leesa had never looked more radiant.

Back at home, Leesa spent much of her time in the nursery's rocking chair with Stephen latched on to her breast. She cradled him with her right arm, and held Sir Arthur Conan Doyle's *The Adventures of Sherlock Holmes* or Herman Wouk's *The Winds of War* in her left hand.

As for that .22 caliber revolver, Leesa brought it to me after the doctor had found Stephen's heartbeat.

"Look what I found," she said.

She told me I must have taken the gun out shooting and left it under the front seat of her car. I couldn't remember shooting it. But I also couldn't believe she had considered using it on herself—even after I popped open the cylinder and found the gun loaded.

Twenty-Six

At 7:45 a.m. on the first Tuesday morning of September 1976, thirty-three men stared at me.

"Good morning, men," I said. "My name is Jackie Deere. You are welcome to call me by my first name. I will call you by your first names. I am not your boss. I am your brother in Christ. I am here to help you learn Hebrew. I will call roll for the first two weeks until I learn your names. I do not take class attendance. If you can learn Hebrew without coming to class, you are welcome to do that. All you have to do to pass the class is pass the tests. It will be difficult to make an A in this class, but you will have to work hard to fail this class. I know that once you graduate, most of you will never look at Hebrew again. I won't punish you because you don't love what I love."

I was a kind and merciful professor. I accepted late assignments without penalty and never got angry with a student who disagreed with me. Once a student snored so loudly that the others burst out laughing. "Shh," I said. "Be quiet or you'll wake him up. He needs the sleep."

I taught five classes of introductory Hebrew grammar. By the end of the first year, if a student asked a question about the infinitive absolute, I could give him an explanation off the top of my head, write out the form for him on the overhead projector, and then tell him to look on page 158, paragraph 129, of the grammar, all without consulting a single note.

I never had to prepare for another Hebrew grammar class.

———

In the late spring of 1977, Leesa woke up, beset by a familiar nausea that had once preceded so much joy. Jim confirmed that Leesa was pregnant.

———

Around that same time, a small Bible church of four hundred people asked me to teach an adult Bible study class on Sunday mornings.

It didn't seem to bother the church, or the seminary, that I hadn't belonged to a house of worship for nine years.

Within a few weeks, people showed up early to save seats and argued over seats—and sometimes otherwise devout, Bible-believing Christians shoved each other out of the way for a place. The class grew to two hundred people. Then the church put a video screen in an overflow room and gave me a part-time position and a salary.

Invitations for exclusive dinners and vacations poured in. Our hosts didn't just know the latest city politics; they knew the politicians. They belonged to the affluent country clubs and lived in homes featured in magazines. They used words like *arbitrage* without the slightest affectation. I knew nothing of politics or business, but I was fascinated rather than intimidated by their conversation and lifestyle.

As I basked in the attention of CEOs and lawyers who were ten or more years older than me, Leesa wilted. She felt dumb and insignificant. I told her she was smart and discerning. I said college degrees didn't mean anything. Intellect, I said, was overrated. Character was what mattered, and she had more goodness than anyone else I knew.

Once again, my words couldn't penetrate her feelings. It was like trying to kill a grizzly bear with a BB gun.

In the car on the way home one night, she extended an invitation into her experience, only to have it snubbed.

"Imagine if you didn't say anything for the whole evening?" she said. "How would you feel?"

"Fine," I said.

But that had never happened. And truth be told, I could not picture any room that held people with whom I could not match wits. It was the sort of invulnerability that blinded me to the wounds of others.

In the homes of senior partners from prestigious law firms, over dinners with prime rib and the latest Napa Valley Cabernets, and amid theological questions tossed my way, Stephen became Leesa's escape route.

Leesa would excuse herself to breastfeed her baby or change his diapers. When she looked into his eyes, it was as if she was back in the serenity of our home, far away from places where her significance came only from the arm on which she had arrived.

Then in the middle of January 1978, our new baby tried so hard to force his way into our world that we braved a North Texas ice storm at midnight to get him to the hospital. But the doctor sent us sliding back home over the ice.

Then our baby refused to come out at all and had to be induced with a Pitocin drip two weeks later.

Another boy.

And I had the perfect name. Our second son would be named David Scott Deere, after my hero David Scott Manley. We would call him Scott.

Twenty-Seven

Despite what the bylaws of any church says about its government, all churches have a boss whose opinion counts the most. Often the boss is not the pastor. In the Bible church where I taught the Sunday school class, the boss was a lawyer in his fifties. He was considered the theologian of the church—until I came.

While my class had more than two hundred people, his class never had more than thirty. What was worse—the laughter from my class rang out down the hallway, mocking him while he tried to teach.

After a year of my Sunday school success, the church boss ambushed me. One of us had to go.

I could have gone peacefully.

Instead, I led an exodus of 120 people—including a contingent of lawyers and oil-rich families out of the church—to the Promised Land of a new and improved church a few miles away.

I had never pastored a church, but I liked people and had trained young people to follow Jesus for the last ten years. I figured that if I stood on a Sunday stage and taught the Bible, people would come. I was right.

In our new church, John and Nancy Snyder became our best friends. John owned an oil company. He and Nancy were new Christians.

They were the rare couple whose grace and humility surpassed exceptional wealth and pedigrees. Leesa felt nourished in their presence.

After we had been friends for more than a year, John mentioned that he once lived back East. Your average Texan does not care much for the East.

"Where back East?" I asked.

"Boston."

"What did you do in Boston?"

"I went to school."

"Oh. Where?"

"Harvard."

"Harvard! Did you get a degree?"

"An MBA."

If I had credentials like that, I would have dropped "Harvard" into the first five minutes of every new conversation.

While John knew about oil and business, Nancy knew about everything else. She became my wine tutor. As she served excellent bottles at each dinner, she taught me the classifications of German, French, Italian, and California wines. She also helped Leesa become a gourmet cook.

After about a year, our new church, Christ Chapel, needed a full-time pastor to oversee the day-to-day operations. I wanted one person, Teddy Kitchens, my close friend since junior high. Teddy was now Ted, all grown-up and dignified. Soon I would grow out of Jackie into the more dignified Jack.

I preferred Ted's company to just about everyone else, but he often had to compensate for my lack of grace. When I handed out harsh corrections to deacons, Ted would correct me.

"Jack, he volunteers for the church," Ted said. "He doesn't have to serve us; he serves us because he loves us. You made him feel small."

Later, I would thank the bruised deacon for his service and apologize.

When people were with me, they felt I was smart. When they were with Ted, they felt important.

Ted's wife, Lynn, also didn't have a college diploma. She and Leesa became constant companions and best friends. While they played competitive racquetball together, they commiserated on the defects of their husbands.

"Ted is such a creep," Lynn told Leesa.

"Not compared to Jack," Leesa said.

Finally Leesa had found homes where she could eat and enjoy a little light outside my shadow.

On June 10, 1980, one of Leesa's most fervent prayers was answered. That evening, a crowd from Christ Chapel came to the hospital to welcome Alese Elizabeth Deere into the world. Leesa lay awake all night, thanking God for Alese. Two days later, we brought her home to a nursery with large bay windows that looked out on the front yard. I had painted her room pink.

All day long, Alese was the undisputed center of attention. Scott saw that Alese had displaced him as the adored baby in the family. A friend held Alese on the couch in the den as Scott disappeared. He returned, holding his red boxing glove by the laces. When he reached Alese, he swung the glove down on the face of his newborn sister with all the force he could muster.

Alese wailed.

We took the kids snow skiing every year and always went on a summer vacation. We spent weekends and holidays at friends' ranches and raised our children in a home filled with thousands of books and one TV.

I wanted the boys to become athletes, but the footballs, basketballs, and baseball gloves lay unused in their closets while they raced around the neighborhood on skateboards and tricked-out bikes.

Leesa showered Alese with Barbie and American dolls and tea parties for her preschool friends.

Each night, Leesa made dinner, and we ate at the kitchen table and talked. One night, when Stephen was in first grade, he asked, "Dad, what does *f—k* mean?"

I choked on the mashed potatoes I had just put in my mouth.

"Yeah," said Scott, who was in kindergarten. "What does *f—k* mean?"

I turned to Leesa in panic. She grinned with a glee that said, *I'm s-o-o-o-o-o glad he asked you and not me.*

When we married, we promised each other that we would be the first to talk to our kids about sex. Neither of us had grown up with adults who could offer honest and frank explanations of sex. We wanted a different experience for our children.

Three-year-old Alese was at the table, providing me with a reason to delay making good on my word.

"Stephen," I said, "I'll tell you later. In the meantime, don't use that word."

Leesa shook her head, as if to say, *You coward!*

The next day I told a counselor what had happened.

"You need to tell him," the counselor said.

"He's six years old, for Pete's sake. I will not explain to him the details of what I do to his mother at night."

"He doesn't want the details. He doesn't even care about sex at this age. He just wants to know that he can ask his daddy anything and get an answer. Besides, if you don't tell him, some kid at school will give him a perverse explanation."

"How much do I tell him?"

"Thirty seconds max—you know, just in and out."

"So when I come home tonight, I take him aside and give him the explanation?"

"No. Don't make a big deal of it. Wait for him to ask again. He will in a day or two."

A few nights later, the boys lay on either side of me in our king-size bed for their bedtime story. While I told the boys the story of David and Goliath, Stephen interrupted.

"Oh, Dad," he said. "You said you would tell me what *f—k* means."

"Sure. Uh, I will. Uh, first of all, don't use that word. It's a swear word like *damn, hell*, or *shit*. The proper word is *sexual intercourse.*"

"Seswual intersource?" asked Stephen.

"That'll do fine, son. This won't be of interest to you now, but one day when you grow up and fall in love and marry a beautiful girl, you will put your penis in her vagina, and it will give both of you great pleasure to express your love for each other in that way. That's what sexual intercourse is."

Stephen said, "Oh, okay. Dad, why wouldn't Saul fight Goliath—cuz he was taller than all the other people?"

Dear God, thank you for that brilliant counselor. Bless him and his practice.

I launched into an explanation of Saul's cowardice. Stephen stopped me after about a minute.

"Da-a-a-a-d," he squealed. "Did you ever do that to Mommy?"

I wanted to scream, "No! No! I'm not a pervert."

That stupid counselor!

Finally, I confessed that I had carnal knowledge of his mother. But I didn't tell him he was the result.

Twenty years earlier, when I dropped my first f-bomb at home, an angry woman with a flyswatter chased me under a kitchen table.

Now, instead of cowering in fear, my boys giggled so much that I couldn't finish the David and Goliath story.

A few weeks after my first sex talk to Stephen and Scott, I sat in my study with commentaries, lexicons, and grammars strewn across my huge desk. At 10 p.m., I had traded the Hebrew text of the Song of Songs for Bob Brister's *Shotgunning: The Art and the Science*. Brister guided me through the mysteries of leading the target when a faculty friend called. I still had my tie on and was deep in conversation when Leesa came in and sat in my lap and surveyed my desktop. Then she leaned in and let her soft brown hair fall across my chest and neck, and her lips brushed my ear. She put her finger on the title of chapter 14 of Brister's book and whispered, "Let's go practice this."

"Gotta go," I said to my friend.

The title of chapter 14: "Velocity and Penetration."

Twenty-Eight

The orange glow of the BMW's dash transfixed me. I had never ridden in any car like the one my friend had just purchased. I got goose bumps as he maneuvered through traffic like a running back on his way to the end zone.

Soon, that car was all I thought about. But I could not afford it on the money I earned from the church and seminary. So I formed a company to import gray market cars from Germany and sell them on the Texas market at a discount. The dollar was on a rampage against the Deutsche Mark, and commercial real estate was on a rampage in Texas. People had piles of cash for extravagances.

By my mid-thirties, I always had two German luxury cars sitting in my driveway. Their combined value nearly equaled that of my four-bedroom home. I had my shirts custom-made and bought Italian shotguns, and it became difficult to tell the difference between me and the lawyers who attended my church. I chased the finer things in life while the best things waited for me at home each night.

"Jack, do you think it's wise to spend so much time selling cars?" asked Dan, one of the elders at my church.

"Dan," I said, "I appreciate your concern, but my car business is the only opportunity I have to be around people who don't know Jesus."

I looked one of my bosses in the eye and told him the real reason I spent so much time buying and selling—and driving—luxury cars was to serve God.

The worst part was that I actually believed it.

As a boy, I had longed to go hunting like some of my friends. But Dad had no time for hobbies, and after he died, I couldn't find anyone to take me. When I became an adult, I pursued the outdoors with abandon and made sure to include my sons.

I made the boys a deal: save $100, and I would put another $100 toward buying them a decent rifle. It took Stephen about three months of raking leaves and mowing lawns to put away the cash. Even with his aversion to work, Scott managed to save about $40. I knew he would never get to the full amount, but I still wanted him to have his own gun. So I took their money and found a couple of Belgium Browning SA-22 rifles—collector guns that would increase in value.

I took Scott on his first quail hunt when he was four years old, as I had done for Stephen. We pulled up at the ranch ten minutes before first light. I let our white and liver colored English pointer, Skipper, out of his kennel. I told Scott to stay by my side as we walked into the wind. Skipper caught the scent of quail in the air and zigzagged across the field. At a patch of grass, he slowed to a creep. Then his body went rigid, his tail high up in the air, his right paw a few inches off the ground, and his nose pointed at the covey of quail we could not see. A perfectly executed point.

"Scott," I whispered, "walk right beside me. Don't move ahead of me. Watch what happens next."

"Okay, Dad."

As we moved past Skipper, the ground in front of us exploded. The air was blurred with more than twenty birds flying out of the grass in all directions. Scott screamed and clutched my leg. I shot a bird, and Skipper ran to fetch it. We repeated that scene all morning.

Scott became used to the routine and rushed ahead of me and Skipper when the dog was on point.

"Scott, don't run in front of Skipper! You'll flush out the birds too soon. Wait for me." I had to warn him over and over. Then he got bored and wandered off.

"Scott, that's a mesquite bush. Its thorns are poisonous. Get your hand back."

Then later, "Scott, that's a rattlesnake hole. Don't put your hand down there."

I corrected Scott the whole day.

At sundown, I loaded Skipper into his kennel and strapped Scott into the front seat. We had borrowed Ted's old Plymouth with a bench front seat. Scott took his seat belt off and scooted over next to me and fastened the middle seat belt. He leaned his blond head on my shoulder.

"Dad," he said, "this has been a great day."

"It has been a great day, Scotty."

"Dad, I'm so tired."

"Me too, Scotty."

"Dad, I'm so thirsty I could drink anything."

He took a moment to ponder what he had just said.

"'Cept potty water, Dad. I wouldn't drink potty water."

I laughed as I pictured the machinery of his literal mind surveying all the potential beverages in his world. Then he saw our Cocker Spaniel drink out of the toilet, forcing him to eat his words.

I put my arm around him and lay my cheek on his head.

"I love you, Scotty boy," I said. "And I wouldn't drink potty water either."

I pulled the car onto the dirt road leading to the highway, and Scott fell asleep on my shoulder. I had corrected him all day long, not because he was defiant, but because he was a little boy who needed to be kept safe. And no matter how many times I had to steer him away from danger, he still brought me joy.

I wondered if that was how God looked at me. It would be wonderful if—against all odds—I could make him that happy.

At the end of his life, C. S. Lewis, who had been surrounded by the theologians of Oxford and Cambridge, wrote, "One is sometimes (not often) glad not to be a great theologian; one might so easily mistake it for being a good Christian."[1]

Not many of us in our seminary heeded that warning.

In my first year at the seminary, a sour and boring professor announced in an imperious tone, "Dallas Seminary is the greatest seminary in the world. If it weren't, I would not be teaching here." My classmates and I laughed at the second sentence. But we all agreed with the first.

Dallas Seminary is the greatest seminary in the world.

That assertion of superiority was reinforced explicitly and implicitly in almost every class I attended and later in every class I taught.

I never saw anyone in my seminary family shudder at the implication of that belief. Since the purpose of the seminary was to train spiritual pastors, we must be the most spiritual people on earth if we were the greatest seminary in the world.

But beneath a facade of coats and ties and conservative haircuts and orthodox theology lay a serpentine underbelly of spiritual superiority. We professors taught our students the Bible while making it harder for them to obey it.

A student once visited my office to discuss a Hebrew assignment, and he also mentioned that he was on probation.

"What kind of probation?" I asked.

"Moral probation," he said.

"What happened?"

"My college girlfriend and I were engaged, and we had sex before we married. We both knew it was wrong, and we felt bad

---

1. C. S. Lewis, *Reflections on the Psalms* (New York: Harcourt, 1958), 57.

about it long after we had married. I confessed it to another student, who told someone on the faculty disciplinary committee, and the committee summoned me to appear before them and put me on probation for a year."

"I am so sorry," I said. "They should have expelled the guy who squealed on you."

James the brother of Jesus wrote, "Therefore confess your sins to each other and pray for each other so that you may be healed" (James 5:16). But here among the self-proclaimed defenders of doctrine, you confessed your sins so that you might be punished.

At the peak of my pride in my academic success and material wealth, I took a yearlong sabbatical and moved our family to the Black Forest in southwest Germany. The intent of the sabbatical was to study whatever I wanted without the burden of teaching. I attended some lectures at the University of Basel, but the seminary would have frowned on my subjects of interest: European history and culture—especially the food, wine, and cars of Europe.

We rented an apartment in the thousand-year-old village of Denzlingen near the city of Freiburg. Our fifth-floor balcony provided spectacular views: vineyards planted on the side of a mountain at the edge of the forest and thunderstorms forming above the mountains.

Within a couple of months, first-grade Scott fell in love with a blonde, blue-eyed girl named Inga, who was in the second grade. She was a few inches taller than him, and from the balcony, I watched their blond heads bob along the walkway to the swimming pool. When I went to Inga's house to fetch Scott one evening after dinner, Inga's mom said, "We think Scott is the most adorable boy we have ever seen. We love having him over."

"We feel the same way about Inga," I said.

When we celebrated Scott's seventh birthday at the Hirschen, a one-star Michelin restaurant in Glottertal, Scott invited only Inga. She gave him a hunting knife with an eight-inch blade.

In the winter, when our German village and its vineyards were covered in snow, I looked up from my book to see Leesa bundling up.

"Where are you going?" I asked.

"For a walk," she said.

"In this? Honey, it's still snowing."

"I know. I enjoy walking in the cold."

She had gone for a two-hour walk every afternoon since we had come to Denzlingen.

"What do you do on these walks?" I asked her.

"I pray," she said.

I went back to my book.

I was proud of her for praying so consistently, but I didn't think to ask what she was praying for.

Leesa had noticed the transition in me. The pursuit of knowledge had supplanted the pursuit of love, and a love of pleasure had replaced my hunger for the eternal things that can't be seen. She also knew a hard heart when she saw one, so she didn't point out that my salvation was no longer the source of joy it had been when we first married.

What she needed was a miracle.

———————

That spring, the mountain runoff of winter's thaw submerged the forest in a sea of oozing mud. As I sat on our balcony reading the latest biography of Mozart, I spotted three boys emerging from the edge of the dark woods. They had their arms over each other's shoulders, singing a German song and laughing. Mud plastered them from head to toe. It took me a second to recognize Scott's blond hair and Stephen's red and gray parka. I assumed the other kid was their friend Thomas.

I grabbed the camera and took a half-dozen shots from the balcony and then ran downstairs for close-ups.

Thomas headed home. I brought the boys into the foyer of our apartment building, and they stripped down to their underwear. I put their muddy clothes and boots into a garbage bag. And it was off to the shower.

As I rejoiced with my muddy boys that day, my mind replayed a twenty-five-year-old memory of the beating that Mom laid on her three boys for playing in the mud of a summer downpour.

Although I pursued the pleasures of life more than the pleasure of my Father, I saw God's great goodness in that memory of Mom's rage.

I should have been in a factory in Texas in a job I hated. I should have been trying to provide for the accidental babies of a misspent youth. I should have been living with a wife I resented for trapping me in a monotonous life, and a wife who hated me for being an angry, absentee, alcoholic husband and father.

Instead we walked through the ruins of Pompeii and climbed to the smoking rim of Vesuvius. We stood under the ceiling of the Sistine Chapel and rode gondolas through the Venetian canals. We toured Mozart's boyhood home in Salzburg and snapped pictures of Alese and Leesa beside the *Mona Lisa* at the Louvre in Paris.

But nothing we did that year made me happier than seeing the distance I'd traveled from the child of a mother who tortured her mud-covered sons to a father who now laughed with his.

Twenty-Nine

In August 1985, we returned to Fort Worth. Our friends met us with glasses of champagne at the baggage claim at the DFW airport. I settled back into the routine of commuting to Dallas two days a week and spending the rest of my time at Christ Chapel. In the evenings, I went for six-mile runs along the Trinity River, and when I came home, Stephen would lie down beside me on the bedroom floor to do sit-ups. Scott liked the camaraderie of stretching out on the floor with his dad and big brother, but he couldn't endure the effort required to crank out more than just a few sit-ups.

When I walked into the boys' bedroom and told them to go clean out the garage, they both said, "Sure, Dad." I looked into the garage ten minutes later to see Stephen sweeping, but Scott had stayed in his bedroom, still playing with his Legos.

"Scott, get in the garage," I said.

"Oh, I'm sorry, Dad," said Scott.

That fall, the elders and I discussed hosting a conference at our church the next year and searched for a speaker. I suggested we invite Dr. John White, my favorite contemporary Christian author. A former professor of psychiatry, White had written many books including *The Fight*, a classic on the challenges of the Christian life; *Parents in Pain*, a book about parenting; and *Eros Defiled*, a book on sex.

Getting White to come to our church was a long shot, so the chairman of our elder board called White's publisher for advice. White's schedule was already full for the next eighteen months, his publisher told us. If he did accept our invitation, he would want to speak on whatever topic he was researching.

The rejection letter arrived a little more than two weeks later.

I didn't want to give up, so I drafted a personal invitation and put it on stationery that identified me as a professor at Dallas Seminary.

Maybe that would get his attention.

A few days later, my phone rang.

"Hello, Jack," said a man with an English accent, "this is John White."

He thanked me for the invitation and said that on second thought, he might be able to work us in after all. What would we like him to speak on?

"Oh, I don't know," I said. "How about something you're writing or researching now?"

He told me he was working on a book about the kingdom of God. To him, Christ's authority made up God's kingdom. He proposed four lectures: "Christ's Authority over Temptation," "Christ's Authority over Sin," "Christ's Authority over Demons," and "Christ's Authority over Disease."

Demons?

Disease?

"You didn't say disease, did you?" I said.

"Yes, I did," he said.

"You don't mean healing, do you?"

Miracles are scattered all throughout the Bible. And they tend to force people into one of three camps—what some label as naturalist, cessationist, and noncessationist.

According to the naturalists, the supernatural events depicted in Scripture never happened but were concocted by the Bible's authors to establish divine authority in a superstitious culture.

The cessationists contend that the miracles in the Bible occurred to establish God's authority. After the completion of the Bible, God ceased performing signs and wonders—at least regularly—because the authority of Scripture had rendered them obsolete.

At the time, I was ensconced in the cessationist camp. I wanted nothing to do with the tongue-speaking, tambourine-rattling, and bouffant-toupee-wearing noncessationists who screamed, sweated, and devil-stomped their way through Sunday morning services, believing that miracles happened and continue to happen today.

Those people made the rest of us Christians look like fools.

———————

But Dr. John White was no fool. He was dead serious about speaking on healing. I gave him a couple of cessationist arguments, but he caught me in an interpretative error.

As I surveyed the other evidence for my position, I saw the dominos fall. Had I really accepted a doctrine without questioning it?

In the end, we agreed to let him speak on healing. But that wasn't enough. Dr. White wanted to pray for the sick. He didn't see the point of talking about something and not doing it.

Over the next several months, I asked questions that I had never considered: Did God heal? Should I expect him to? Who did he heal? And why? I opened the Bible, searching for answers—this time with fresh eyes.

I examined every healing story in the New Testament, asking one simple question: "God, why did you do this?" Then I used those New Testament stories to evaluate the arsenal of arguments I had collected for why miracles had ceased. After four months, I knew I had no reason to believe that God had stopped healing, and I had no choice but to pray for the sick, just as Scripture commanded.

On a Saturday afternoon in April 1986, White presented a lecture to 350 people on healing; it was so bland that I could have given it at Dallas Seminary without raising anyone's blood pressure. He took questions afterward.

"Do you speak in tongues?" the first questioner asked.

The lecture had been on healing, not tongues. I thought it was a rude incursion into Dr. White's private life. The questioner was a member of our church and looked up to me. I led a Bible study downtown that he attended. And I'd also taught him to despise Pentecostals.

"No," White said.

After about thirty minutes, White concluded the question-and-answer period. The time to pray for people had arrived. He invited anyone who wanted prayer to come to the front of the sanctuary, and a line of more than fifty people formed. I stood behind him to observe the proper way to pray for the sick, thinking I might pick up some good technique.

Instead a window opened, disclosing the hurts of people I had helped gather but did not know well enough to sense their pain.

The wife of a wealthy art dealer knelt on our stage and wept.

"I don't feel like anyone in the world loves me except for my husband," she said.

A thirty-year-old man fell to his knees and cried.

"I'm so eaten up with jealousy and envy," he said. "All my friends have passed me by and have better jobs."

Then a woman who was chronically depressed came forward and said that she now understood the true nature of her problems.

"I lust after the approval of men," she said.

"Let's pray for you then," said Dr. White.

He laid his right hand on her shoulder and prayed, "Lord, Linda does not feel your affection. Let her feel how much you love her right now."

I was amazed at Dr. White's insight. He went right to the heart of her problem. She lusted after men's approval because she did not feel the affection of her God. I had known her for years and offered her lots of counsel, but I had never seen the root of her suffering.

"And Lord," White prayed, "if there be any darkness manipulating this pain, I pray you would make it leave now."

Her head bobbed up and down. The veins, tendons, and muscles of her neck hardened, creating conduits for an ear-splitting scream that I thought might shatter the sanctuary's windows.

Thirty

With the woman's scream, the sanctuary surged with terror. The only person who lacked fear was Dr. White, who had seen this before and knew what to do.

"In the name of Jesus, be at peace," he said. The screaming stopped.

I woke up the next morning in the dark and wondered how far the shrieking had traveled. About 350 people attended our church, which is nowhere near megachurch numbers, but they were the right kind of people: wealthy and dignified.

What we had invited into our midst was undignified and unconcerned with money. How long would it take for word to spread and for us to be ridiculed?

So I did something I would have mocked a year earlier. In the dark, I asked God to speak to me, opened my Bible, and let my finger fall randomly on the page. It landed on Luke's story of the Gerasene demoniac, the man whom Jesus had freed of thousands of demons. At the end of the episode, the people of the Gerasene region were overcome with fear and asked Jesus to leave (Luke 8:26–39).

God had come to our church in power to free a woman from demonic oppression, and I woke up ready to ask God not to come back in that way. But not anymore.

Ted picked me up that morning. We drove west on Interstate 30, passing the glass skyscrapers of downtown Fort Worth on the way to the church we both had built.

Ted had that same fearful look on his face that I had awakened with.

"Ted, everything will be okay. That really was God yesterday," I said. "You don't have to worry."

Ted was unmoved by my experience in Luke 8 that morning, and when I couldn't get that light to come back in his eyes, I grew frustrated.

That frustration would soon turn into anger.

Leesa and I grew addicted to the experience of laying hands on people as Jesus did, asking God to make wrong things right in their bodies, minds, and souls. Regardless of the outcome, people felt loved.

I put out the word that we were now taking appointments for prayer during the week and that I needed volunteers to join a healing team. Four women signed up first—the wives of some of my best friends in the church. Their husbands did not share their enthusiasm.

One of our members, Ruth, called to say an angiogram had revealed an aneurysm inside her head. The walls of a blood vessel had stretched so thin that the next pump of blood could cause them to explode. Her brain was a time bomb.

Ruth's husband had divorced her. She was estranged from her children. When Leesa, a woman from the healing team, and I arrived at her home, she offered us iced tea and cookies, and I wondered if we were her first visitors in a long time.

As far as we could tell, nothing happened when we put our hands on her head and asked God to heal the aneurysm. But a few days later, Ruth called, her voice still weak from the anesthesia.

"Jack, I've been healed," she said.

"What?"

"I have been healed," she repeated.

The physicians cancelled the surgery because a second angiogram revealed that the aneurysm had vanished. Her doctor said he had never witnessed anything like it.

I got rid of my car business. I stopped buying expensive clothes. The focus of my sermons changed. No longer did I point to spiritual disciplines that improved your life. I emphasized God's love.

Those around me noticed.

"I can't believe how much you've changed," people said to me.

It was true. I had changed. I prayed for people now instead of being content to teach them. In my mind, I thought I was more spiritual than ever. But feeling loved by God and thinking that I'm spiritual is the difference between precious metal and fool's gold.

In an experience of God's affection, I feel special in the face of my sin. When I feel spiritual, I am blind to my sin. One feeling leads to superiority, and the other leads to gratitude and humility.

The people who feel the most spiritual are the people who do the most damage in life, like the religious leaders who crucified Christ.

"The vain person wants praise, applause, admiration, too much and is always angling for it," C. S. Lewis wrote. "It is a fault, but a childlike and even (in an odd way) a humble fault. It shows . . . you value other people enough to want them to look at you. The real black, diabolical Pride comes when you look down on others so much that you do not care what they think of you."[1]

I had read that passage in Lewis's *Mere Christianity* dozens of times. And yet I did not stop to ask why it was so easy for me to disregard the opinions of others.

Was it because I thought so much of God? Or so little of others? Or both?

---

1. Lewis, *Mere Christianity*, 112–13.

Perhaps we always vacillate between the light and the illusion of light from one moment to the next.

The trick is to recognize the transition.

For years, I had stood on my Sunday morning stage and convinced people that God no longer healed or spoke outside the pages of the Bible. Now I proclaimed the opposite—a seamless shift for me, a dizzying one for others.

The changes taking place within me were so profound that I couldn't see the heads spinning all around me.

Ted expected me to be reasonable and patient. I expected him, and everyone else, to get in line. When Ted balked, I told him he was like the Gerasenes who told Jesus to leave.

While some of our members praised the change in me, others went to Ted, demanding that he account for the damage I had done. Factions formed. Wives gathered around me; their husbands coalesced around Ted.

Despite the fault lines, my confidence remained unshakable. If someone had to leave, I assumed it would be Ted.

Thirty-One

In the early twentieth century in different parts of the world—from Azusa Street in Los Angeles to New Quay in South Wales—a new phenomenon infused churches, especially those of the working poor.

People ran, jumped, shook all over, and spun around in circles. They fell on the floor, jerked, kicked, and sometimes lay still for hours on end. There were reports of healings, visions, and speaking in other tongues.

Some called it the work of the Holy Spirit; others dubbed it madness.

I don't know why it couldn't have been a mixture of both. Whatever the case, the Pentecostal movement was born. The Pentecostals held similar beliefs to other Christians: Scripture was without error. Jesus' death paid for sin. The path to heaven was through accepting that payment.

The Pentecostals differed from their mainstream brethren in that they embraced direct encounters with the Holy Spirit as if they were an everyday part of life. They didn't see themselves any differently from those first Christians on whom the Holy Spirit descended on the Day of Pentecost in the second chapter of Acts.

For what it's worth, Acts also includes critics who questioned the sanity and sobriety of those who had fallen under the Spirit's power.

Fifty years later, against the backdrop of Vietnam and Woodstock, the hippies of Southern California began to see visions and experience healings and convert en masse to Christianity, giving rise to the Jesus Movement—or the "second wave" of the Spirit's outpouring. They were called "the charismatics" after their beliefs in the miraculous charismatic gifts of the Spirit.

Unlike some Pentecostals, adherents of this new move of the Spirit didn't forbid the use of electric guitars and drums in church services. The charismatic worship bands produced a new style of worship music that sometimes rivaled the best contemporary rock & roll. And instead of forming a new denomination, the charismatic movement infiltrated all denominations.

The charismatic movement also promoted speaking in tongues, but not as dogmatically as the Pentecostals.

As the 1960s drew to a close in Southern California, Costa Mesa's Calvary Chapel, led by Chuck Smith, became the hub of the Jesus Movement. Many young charismatic pastors brought their churches into Calvary Chapel's association.

One of those churches was pastored by a redheaded young man who had encountered Jesus just a few years earlier.

His name was John Wimber.

Wimber came from tainted stock: alcoholic farmers in Missouri who had lost their farms in the Great Depression. They loaded their possessions on a caravan of old cars and trucks and headed west to the orange groves of Southern California.

From an early age, Wimber's musical talent made him stand out. His mom stretched her dollars for instruments and lessons, and by 1962, the twenty-nine-year-old was the keyboard player for a band he had formed called the Paramours—the precursor to The Righteous Brothers.

As his professional life soared, his marriage disintegrated.

Wimber's wife, Carol, had left with their four children and planned to divorce him. But an invitation led them to a small Bible study in Yorba Linda, California, led by a fifty-year-old welder named Gunner.

Nine years earlier, a farmhand had tried to rape Gunner's sixteen-year-old daughter, Ruby, while she babysat the children of neighboring citrus growers. The boy, Billy Rupp, shot Ruby in the back as she fled, killing her. The locals formed a search party.

"It's lucky I found him first," Gunner said, "or the men would have killed him." Gunner forgave Billy, visited him in jail, and led him into a relationship with Christ before the state of California executed him. A columnist from the *Los Angeles Times* started his article on Gunner by saying, "I think I've just met my first Christian."

After a few months into the Bible study, John and Carol tried to pray out loud a prayer of surrender to Jesus, but they fell to the floor, sobbing and shaking. As he wept, John worried about how foolish he looked. A scene from his youth flashed in his mind. He had gone to Pershing Square in Los Angeles to borrow money from a drug dealer. As John scanned the sea of faces, a man walked by, wearing a sandwich board that read, "I'M A FOOL FOR CHRIST."

You sure are, thought John. As the man walked past, John saw the question on the back of the board.

"WHOSE FOOL ARE YOU?" it read.

Now John felt foolish for feeling foolish. "I'll be your fool the rest of my life," he promised God.

John gave up his life in the music business, and two of his band members, Bobby Hatfield and Bill Medley, formed their own group, The Righteous Brothers. They went on to a string of top ten hits, some of which John had arranged.

John read the Bible and loved it, especially the stories of the miracles of Jesus. He did not love church. The music was terrible, and the sermons put him to sleep. After a few months, John had only one question: "When do we get to do the stuff?"

"What stuff?" the pastor asked.

When the pastor figured out that John meant the healings and miracles of the Bible, he told him that Christians don't do that anymore.

"Well, what do you do?" asked John.

"Just what you saw this morning," said the pastor.

"You mean I gave up drugs for this?"

Wimber would eventually lead a small Bible study that became a Calvary Chapel church.

He insisted on "doing the stuff." After a while, some of the same kinds of Azusa manifestations occurred among his flock, and John had to leave the Calvary Chapel group. He joined a small group of churches called the Vineyard. John became the leader, and that little group of churches became the vanguard of a new movement of churches—the "third wave" of the Spirit.

Before John White left my church, he told me he had spent the last seven months in Anaheim, California, medically documenting healings that had occurred at the Vineyard Christian Fellowship. He told me to meet the pastor, John Wimber, if I ever had the chance. He said Wimber was a good man who was committed to the Scriptures and was the most gifted healer he had ever met.

Two weeks after John White left my church, Wimber flew in from California for three days of meetings in a Southern Baptist church in Fort Worth. After the time of singing ended, a man with white hair and a white beard with traces of red walked out onto the stage. He wore khakis, jogging shoes, and the kind of loose-fitting, untucked shirt that older men wear to conceal their weight.

His face always seemed lit up like he was about to crack a joke.

He reminded me of a Young Life leader.

John shattered all my stereotypes of faith healers. He made no promises, didn't push speaking in tongues, didn't ask for money.

He told crowds that others in his church were better at praying for the sick than he was. He kept no entourage to protect him from the people who swarmed around him after he spoke. He stayed for hours after the message, laying hands on one person after another.

Leesa and I introduced ourselves to Wimber after the meeting in Fort Worth.

A week later, he called me from California with a warning.

"Jack, you are sitting on top of a powder keg," he said. "If you go any further with healing or with me, you will probably lose your church and your career at Dallas Seminary."

"My course is set," I told him, "no matter the cost."

In May 1987, Wimber flew Leesa and me to Anaheim to spend a few days at the Vineyard, located in a warehouse in an industrial section of town. It was the opposite of the cathedrals I had toured in Europe that were adorned with ornate stone carvings and gold-plated statues.

Long counters ran down the walls on the way to the auditorium, and behind them stood people to answer questions about the church and its many ministries.

The auditorium could seat more than three thousand people. Ten minutes before the Sunday morning service began, the room was already filled. I was the only person wearing a tie.

Wimber played the keyboard that morning, and I felt God come into the room from the first note. People didn't merely sing; they worshiped, raising their hands—a universal sign of surrender—to contemporary music, with simple personal lines like, "I love you, Lord."

To my right, I saw a young woman fall to her knees on the front row. Tears rolled down her cheeks. She lifted up her hands. At first I felt revulsion, and then I wondered if she was repenting, like the prostitute who washed Jesus' feet with her tears. Or maybe

God had simply overwhelmed her with his love. Whatever the case, in that moment, she didn't care what I or anybody else thought.

I wished I could be so free.

After the Sunday service, John and Carol took us out for lunch. When we pulled back into the church parking lot after lunch, hundreds of cars were still parked. I started to point him in the direction of our car, but he turned right in toward it. Then he made a second turn toward it. *How is it*, I wondered, *that he knows where we parked without me telling him?*

When he pulled into an empty spot near our car, a profound fear swept through me. *Could he see into my soul?*

Then he said, "I want to take you to our bookstore and get some tapes and books for you."

I laughed out loud.

"What's so funny?" asked John.

"We are parked right there. I thought you were guided supernaturally to our car."

"Carol, did you hear that? Jack knows what a holy person I am."

Then everyone laughed.

From its inception, no one doubted that I determined our church's direction. But all too often, leaders are too busy looking ahead to see the condition of the people behind them, let alone care for them. Caring for people was Ted's specialty.

Now Ted not only had to calm down people I had inflamed, but he had to argue with me about why they shouldn't be inflamed. And he had to endure me calling him a people pleaser.

Over the course of a few months, I dismantled a friendship that had taken twenty-five years to build. I had no idea what I was doing, but Ted did. One weekend while he was away at a marriage conference in Dallas, he lamented the loss of our friendship and called me to apologize for a recent clash.

"Jack, I'm so sorry for what I said to you the other day," he said. "Please forgive me."

Instead of holding fast to that olive branch, I smashed it over my knee.

"Ted, your disobedience to God in this matter is clear to me," I said. "You don't need to repent to me; you need to repent to God."

Ted said good-bye and hung up. In their hotel, he looked at Lynn and wept.

Thirty-Two

In my seminary office, a student sat across from my desk and droned on about why I should accept a late assignment. Suddenly he disappeared. I was transported to some strange place. I couldn't see him or hear him, and I lost any awareness of my body. Then I saw the word PORNOGRAPHY in bold, black capital letters. It lasted long enough for me to realize I hadn't concocted the trance.

When I returned to my office, I took a deep breath, looked into his eyes, and blurted out, "Are you into pornography?" The look in his eyes told me he was. It also told me he was about to lie about it.

"Before you say anything, I want you know I will never tell anyone your name. You won't get into any trouble. I think the Lord has told me you're into pornography because he wants to set you free."

"Yes," he said. He had picked up the habit as a teenager and never told anyone.

"Can I pray for you?" I asked.

I stood beside his chair and put my hand on his shoulder. I silently asked God to speak to me about this young man, as Wimber had taught me to do.

"There is more here than pornography, isn't there?" I said.

He lay his head on my desk and pounded it with his fist. I watched his tears run off the desk and soak into the carpet.

"I'm so ashamed," he whispered. "I'm so ashamed. I'm so ashamed."

Then he told me his shame. I put my hand back on his shoulder and prayed for God to set him free. He thanked me and left.

That evening, as I walked past the library, he ran up to me and hugged me.

"Something left me," he said. "I feel different."

For ten years after that, I received messages from him, letting me know the weight that had lifted hadn't returned.

As those experiences became more frequent, my battles with Ted intensified, politicizing every decision.

The elder board at Christ Chapel consisted of three pastors who graduated from Dallas Seminary and four businessmen. We had agreed to not make significant decisions unless the vote was unanimous. Now it was time to consider adding another elder. A man named Don had been nominated. He met all the criteria: good father, good husband, knew the Bible.

The vote was six for and one against.

"Jack, why can't you vote for Don?" asked the chairman.

"I just don't feel right about making him an elder at this time."

Everyone at the table knew it was a lie. Don's sympathies lay with Ted, not me. His appointment would have tipped the balance of power.

With such open duplicity, I did more to undermine myself than Don could ever have.

By the spring of 1987, I refused to face the obvious fact that one of us would have to resign. As the founder, I envisioned building the perfect church—one that melded biblical literacy with the supernatural gifts of the Spirit and passionate worship. So at the peak of our power struggle, I invited Ted and Lynn to our house for dinner, so I could have another shot to persuade him to come over to my side.

Instead of wooing him with an apology, I tried to bludgeon him with fear.

"I'm going to speak to crowds of people and fill stadiums," I said. "Our church will explode. You'll be jealous that your unbelief in God's supernatural power kept you on the sidelines."

At that moment, Ted knew our friendship had ended. What I hadn't considered was that I had also ended Leesa's relationship with Lynn.

It was our last dinner.

———

That June, I went to the church for an elder meeting at two in the afternoon. The first thing I noticed was that Ted wasn't there. Then I saw that some of the men were reluctant to look me in the eye. As I sat down, my stomach tightened.

"Jack, we can't go on like this," the chairman said. "There doesn't seem to be any way to reconcile the rift in our church."

I was about to tell him I agreed.

Then he said, "We think you should resign."

I looked at Bill, an elder who had spent hours with me praying for people, who had gone to Wimber conferences with me, who believed exactly what I believed, and who had embraced my vision of the perfect church.

"Bill, do you think I should resign?" I said. "Do you agree with them?"

"I do, Jack. I do," he said. "There is no other way."

One of us had to go. It had come down to a choice between two men who, up until that point, had perfectly complemented each other.

One always wanted to chart a bold course, but frequently confused courage with pride and ignored all the wounds he inflicted.

The other cared for people, but could care too much about what they thought.

A leader. Or a pastor.

I can say this now. I couldn't then.

They chose wisely.

Thirty-Three

At the start of my eleventh year of teaching, a student sat across from my desk and leveled an insult that I would have never uttered as a student.

"Dr. Deere, you are ruining the course," he said. "You obviously know all the material. But you are shortchanging us. You are far too devotional in class. I go to church for my spiritual life. I come to your Old Testament Introduction course to learn how to fight against the liberals."

He was right. I had become the kind of professor I despised as a student. But I couldn't help it.

I had lost the desire to teach languages my students would never use and tactics for a war with the liberals they would never fight.

No one in my church ever asked me whether Moses wrote the first five books of the Bible or if it was some scribe or scribal school that compiled the Torah in the fifth century BCE. And yet I had to convince my students they should know the ins and outs of each side of the argument.

I should have been happy. I still loved languages and academic theology. I had tenure. I could teach any class I wanted. The library would purchase any book I wanted. The only papers I had to grade were master's theses and doctoral dissertations. My job was effortless.

As I learned more about the gifts, the one I saw the least examples of was prophecy—the supernatural ability to predict the future and reveal things hidden in the present.

Then in the fall of 1987, I spoke at a Presbyterian church in Kansas City, and a man in the audience punctuated my points with shouts of "Glory!" After the meeting, we met.

"I'm Mike Bickle," said the thirty-three-year-old leader of "the Kansas City prophets."

He was built like a short, powerful fullback who ran over linebackers, and he had a deep, resonant voice.

Mike had wanted to go to Dallas Seminary, but he had to drop out of college to care for his brother Pat, who had broken his neck in a high school football game and was now a quadriplegic.

"Would you like to meet some of our prophetic people in the morning?" Mike asked me.

"Sure," I said.

Wimber had warned me earlier about the company Bickle kept: "I know those guys, Jack. I like Mike Bickle, but those prophets are nothing special. God gave you a good mind. Don't go up there and get deceived."

At eight o'clock the next morning, Leesa and I, along with five of our friends from Fort Worth, walked into a small room in the basement of the church. At the door, I met a six-foot-tall man with a full salt-and-pepper beard and deep-set, spooky eyes.

"Oh, I didn't expect to see you here this morning," he said.

Already I did not like him.

"What do you mean?" I said. "I don't even know you."

"Well, I know you. I saw you in a dream eight nights ago. I thought it was important, so I wrote it down. Would you like me to tell you what the Lord showed me about you?"

"Sure," I said.

Twelve of us sat in a circle in orange plastic chairs that clashed with the bright green carpet.

"Your father dropped the ball on you," he said.

True, but he could have found that out with just a little research.

"You are in a conflict. You think there are only three people on your side, but there are five more on your side you don't know about."

Only Leesa knew about this conflict and the three people on my side. Now he had my attention, but my expression remained flat.

"When you were young, God gave you athletic ability, but he allowed you to be frustrated in the use of that ability so you would channel all your energy into building an intellectual kingdom," he said. "You are at the top of your kingdom now, and you are heartsick. All this frustration has been necessary for you to fulfill the assignment that God has for your life."

Those words overwhelmed me, but all he saw was a blank stare on my face.

"You have a prayer. It's actually the dream of your heart," he said.

Then he told me the prayer I prayed that morning in our hotel room, the prayer I prayed every morning.

He said, "God said to tell you that the dream is from him and he'll answer your prayer."

Inside, I cried. It took every bit of self-control I had to hold on to that blank stare as my mind reeled and my heart raced.

"Thanks," I said.

After the meeting, Mike asked, "Was anything that John Paul said true?"

"Every bit of it was true."

"But your face said none of it was true."

I told him I had been warned.

That year, I attended Vineyard conferences around the country. John paid Leesa's and my way. After an evening session at a conference in Ohio, I stood next to John to watch him while he answered questions and prayed for people. A young woman asked me, "Are you with him?"

"Yes," I said.

"Would you give him this?" she asked as she handed me a note.

"Sure. What does it say?" I asked.

She told me she was born with a split spinal cord—*diastematomyelia* in doctor-speak. At twenty-nine, she was scheduled for surgery to repair the condition. The surgery could have paralyzed her or even taken her life. Wimber prayed for her nine months earlier at a conference in San Diego. When she went back to the doctor, she had one spinal cord.

A line of at least two dozen people stretched out from John. She knew he was tired and didn't want to bother him. She wanted him to know that God had healed her.

At midnight, John and I sat in a restaurant eating chili, coleslaw, and French fries. I tried to give him the note. "What does it say?" he asked. I told him.

"Oh, I remember her. That's great," he said and took another bite of coleslaw—and he didn't mention it again.

At the time, the most conservative evangelicals believed that the charismatic gifts described in Scripture had ceased. To some, the third-wave movement resembled an infection, and I was now at a key entry point.

If someone like Wimber could dupe a tenured professor at Dallas Theological Seminary into believing in the gifts, no one was safe. The ecclesiastical power brokers were nervous, and in October 1987, they convinced Don Campbell, the seminary's third president, to apply the pressure.

"Jack, nine out of the last ten days, I've had calls from our constituency complaining about you," Campbell told me over lunch. "Calls from within the country, and even from outside the country. People want to know how I can continue to let you remain on the faculty when you are so obviously in sympathy with a man like John Wimber."

"You're between a rock and a hard place," I said. "I'm sorry to be the cause of it."

The next month, Campbell gave me a choice: renounce my friendship with Wimber, or resign from Dallas Seminary.

After that interview, a two-page memo appeared in our faculty boxes. The second page was titled "Implications for the Faculty of the Doctrinal Statement's Article on Spiritual Gifts and the Charismatic Movement."

From that time on, the faculty had to segregate themselves not only from charismatics but also from "charismatic-type" people.

The memo was not signed.

The fifth implication of the doctrinal statement was aimed at me: "Faculty members are expected to avoid promoting—on or off campus—charismatic or charismatic-type practices, persons, or movements."

I had never mentioned Wimber's name on campus. But my friendship with him off campus was considered promoting a "charismatic-type" person. We all knew what a charismatic was, but what was a charismatic-type? It was John Wimber. Presumably, it was also me.

While I was a professor, I had been friends with alcoholics and agnostics, addicts and attorneys, atheists and adulterers, and even the owner of a liquor store. But now my friendship with a "charismatic-type" Christian had put the purity of Dallas Seminary at risk.

I was given thirty days to renounce Wimber or resign.

When my time ran out, I walked into Don Campbell's office.

"I will not resign," I said. "I will not renounce Wimber. I leave the matter in your hands. Do what you think will please God. I will not contest your decision."

Dr. Campbell fired me for doctrinal deviation, not for a deviant friendship.

My last day at the seminary was December 18, 1987. Twenty-two years earlier on December 18, God had found me in a bedroom in the middle of the night in a little house on the east side of Fort Worth. How odd.

I came home that Friday evening, adrift for the first time in twenty-two years. My well-defined life was gone. Wimber was right. It was a powder keg.

Our dining room glowed in candlelight. Leesa had set the table for one of her French dinners. New friends would be joining us. At my seat, Leesa had placed our three local newspapers, the *Fort Worth Star-Telegram*, the *Dallas Morning News*, and the *Dallas Times Herald*. I was mentioned by name in each of them—and cast as David versus the institutional Goliath.

Before dinner, a friend called to say he had prayed for me that morning. Haggai 2:18–19 popped into his mind. When we hung up, I turned to Haggai 2:18–19, which read, "From this day on, from this twenty-fourth day of the ninth month . . . From this day on I will bless you." I went into the study and pulled a biblical chronology book off the shelf. I looked up Haggai's twenty-fourth day of the ninth month.

It was 520 BC, December 18.

Now I understood.

None of this had been an accident.

Thirty-Four

In May 1988, I attended a conference in Greenville, South Carolina, where Mike Bickle spoke on "passion for Jesus." Until that message, I had never heard the phrase "passion for Jesus."

I had never prayed for my feelings. If I thought about my feelings at all, it was about a strategy to defeat them.

Mike stood on a stage that night with no notes, only an open Bible. In his reverberant voice, he told us that the apostle John was Jesus' best friend, who only referred to himself as "the disciple whom Jesus loved." And in that love, John found his identity and his self-worth—not in his service.

Mike had more authority than any teacher I had ever heard. He did not proclaim a doctrine that he had studied; he revealed the power of a truth that lived in him. I wanted the spiritual life I saw in him. I wanted his passion for God. I hadn't felt that way about anyone since Scott Manley had been yanked out of my life.

Mike read John 17:26 to us, where Jesus prayed, "[Father,] I have made you known to them [the apostles], and will continue to make you known in order that the love you have for me may be in them and that I myself may be in them."

"It takes God to love God," Mike said. I had never heard anyone say it like that. Then he turned the verse into his own prayer: "Father, grant me a work of the Holy Spirit to love the Son of God like you love him"—a prayer that was too profound not to steal.

I have uttered it every night since.

We moved to Anaheim, California, in September 1988, and I joined the staff of the Vineyard Christian Fellowship of Anaheim. John bought us a four-bedroom home about twenty minutes from the church and remodeled it to our taste. Not long after we moved in, Scott and I were alone in the house on a Saturday.

At lunchtime, I came out of my bedroom, where I had been reading. As I walked down the hall, I heard Scott talking to someone. I stopped to eavesdrop on Scott and this mystery guest.

I heard a high-pitched voice say, "Please don't cut me."

"I have to cut you," said Scott. "You're going on my sandwich."

"No, please," begged the tomato. "Just take the lettuce instead."

Then my aspiring ventriloquist let out a sound like a piglet ripped away from its mother.

"Lettuce, you're next," announced Scott, intoning the executioner.

"You don't want me," said the lettuce. "I'm wilted."

"Liar! I'm ripping you."

The lettuce screamed its last scream.

Then the bread begged in vain not to be smothered with mayonnaise.

I would have laughed out loud, but I wanted to keep listening. He kept up the charade until he took the first bite of his ham and cheese sandwich.

If you wanted a detailed explanation of the structure of the Book of Acts, you wouldn't get it at the Vineyard. But if you spent time at John's church, you would see glimpses of how Christians in that day lived.

Thousands of volunteers prayed for the sick, cared for the poor and homeless, served prisoners and their families, and gathered in homes each week to celebrate their experiences of God together and to love one another.

John took me all over the world for Vineyard conferences. He put me on a stage in front of thousands and introduced me to key leaders in a host of far-flung countries.

At the time, I took his generosity for granted, believing that I had earned the platform he provided. Yet I still looked up to him.

When I debated a prominent theologian in front of five hundred of his students, John showed up to watch. My opponent had already prejudged me. He thought I believed tongue speaking was the essential ingredient to a deep spiritual life and that God wanted to heal everyone. I surprised him when I told him I did not believe those things.

Then he made a critical biblical error, exposing his jugular. Years earlier I could not have passed up the opportunity. But as I pondered the prospect of humiliating him, I realized I had a choice. Win the debate, or win a potential friend. I chose the latter, and I began to treat the event more like a discussion than a fencing match.

After the debate, he invited me to give lectures to his students.

Afterward, John, Leesa, and I rode home together.

"Jack," he said, "I'm proud of you. You were great tonight. You were kind."

I felt the same way I did after Scott Manley told me I had done an excellent job telling my story.

———

Scott had never done well in school. He couldn't sit still and routinely wound up in the classrooms of the most rigid teachers. At the small elementary school near our home, the principal suspended him several times—once for egging the building during Christmas break.

We found another place for him, a specialized learning center that recognized not all students flourish in the same kind of environment. His teacher loved him, but he brought her to tears.

While Leesa and I ministered at lengthy Vineyard services and conferences, Stephen and Scott would hang out with the church receptionists at the front desk. One played the guitar and gave Stephen free lessons. Another had been stabbed while he served as a missionary on the streets of Hollywood. Another studied to be a chiropractor and regaled the boys with stories about how individual vertebrae affected all the different parts of the body.

During a conference one night, the would-be chiropractor pulled me aside.

"Jack, I just saw Scott, and he was high."

"How do you know he was high?" I asked.

"He was glassy-eyed and a little out of it."

"Scott's always a little out of it, but he wouldn't smoke marijuana," I said.

"Jack, all I can tell you is that I used to get high," he said. "He's definitely high."

I had never taken drugs. I didn't even know what marijuana smelled like. I didn't consider that familiarity breeds recognition, nor that the receptionist had no motive to exaggerate or lie to one of his bosses.

About an hour later, Scott found me in the foyer.

"Dad, Bob said I was high on pot," Scott said. "Why would he say that? You know I'd never do pot."

"I don't know, Scott. Don't worry. I didn't believe him."

It was the kind of brilliant preemptive strike that I would continue to witness as Scott grew. He couldn't perform long division to save his life, but he intuitively understood a pillar truth of crisis communications: the best way to kill a story is to tell it without being asked.

Thirty-Five

On the weekends, I followed John's three sons into the Mojave Desert. I brought my pistols, rifles, and shotguns and offered advice on shooting. They brought their motorcycles and taught my sons how to traverse canyons.

I spent the evenings before Christmas of 1991 shopping for dirt bikes for my boys. One night, I came home to find Leesa inconsolable, holding her face in her hands. She couldn't speak or even look up. Alese had one arm around her mom.

"What happened?" I asked.

She told me that earlier that night, Scott had a nosebleed. Leesa tried to get him to tilt his head back and put pressure on it with a rag. He just wanted to let it bleed into a cup while he watched TV. They argued. The cup was knocked over. And Scott raged.

He called Leesa something a son should never say to his mother.

"Where is he?"

"In his bedroom."

When I threw open Scott's bedroom door, he jumped off his waterbed. I grabbed my thirteen-year-old son by his shirt and lifted him off the floor, his head level with my head.

"What did you call your mother?" I yelled.

"Dad, please."

"Dad? You call my wife a motherf—er and think you can call me Dad?" I yelled.

I threw him on his waterbed. I never hurt him physically. But I wanted him to think I was going to hurt him.

Then I pronounced him indefinitely grounded.

I forgot all about my own story of the "damn shittin' rat," the backroom, and my dad's mercy.

Publicly, John was always gracious, even to his critics, but he could be cranky with his inner circle. He complained that I spent too much of the church's money on books or long-distance calls when we were out of the country. It irked John when I acted more like a partner than a subordinate, like the time I took my family on a three-week vacation to Hawaii without asking John or telling anyone else how long I would be gone.

He had made me a household name in congregations all over the country. I was the chief theologian in a movement of more than five hundred churches. As usual, I tended to discount all those gifts, and as time revealed more of John's flaws, I turned into the rebellious son, provoking my spiritual father to fury behind closed doors.

Sometimes he devastated me. But we always apologized after a day or two.

As my fourth year ran out, so did our patience for one another. The subject of our breaking point was silly: where I planned to spend my vacation.

A handful of the Vineyard's top leaders had acquired John's love of food along with his love of people. I was one of them. However, I longed for the thirty-two-inch waist I'd had when we returned from Europe six years earlier. A wealthy businessman in the church offered me a free month in Santa Monica at what was essentially a fat camp for rich people.

John forbade me to go. I never learned the real reason. But the

Anaheim Vineyard was in the middle of a fund-raising campaign for a new building. I assumed he just wanted my fat camp money. But I couldn't say that.

I called him controlling.

He blew up, and when I made it clear that I had been inoculated to his anger, he made it clear that I had to go.

I spent my last days as a California resident running fourteen miles a day up and down the beach and pretending to enjoy food stripped of salt and fat.

———————

In May 1992, Leesa put Alese and two Cocker Spaniels, Missy and Susie May, into a Camry, and I put Stephen and Scott into a Suburban, and we drove the cars that John had bought us back to the city of my birth.

My name remained prominent in the movement John had created and among other churches where he had given me a platform. Speaking invitations poured in. I worked on a book.

Five months after we returned to Fort Worth, I picked up a ringing phone in the home we had rented. I was shocked to hear the voice on the other end.

It was John.

"Jack, I am so sorry," he said. "I did not want our first call to be like this. I just found out that a youth worker sexually molested Scott and another pastor's son."

The worker's name was Chris. He was a thirty-year-old financial adviser with no knowledge of finance, no money, and the maturity of a high school kid.

After the phone call, I went into Scott's room.

"Scott, I just talked to John Wimber," I said. "He told me about Chris. It's very important that you don't lie to me now."

"Okay," said Scott.

"What did you and Chris do?"

"Everything but kiss."

I had counseled men who had been molested as preteens and teens. I knew how sexual assault created sexual confusion. I told Scott it wasn't his fault. He had been taken advantage of. I couldn't tell if he believed me.

We attended Restoration, a church of more than two thousand on Sundays, near Fort Worth. At the conclusion of a Sunday service, the pastor, Doug White, said he thought God had spoken to him about someone in the audience.

"There is a young man here today who thinks he has AIDS, but you don't," White said. "Satan is lying to you."

Later that afternoon, Scott said to me, "Dad, I was the young man. I feel free now."

Thirty-Six

Although Scott had been delivered from the fear of AIDS, some unnamed afflictions still clung to him. Leesa found marijuana in his sock drawer. Then she got a phone call that he had been arrested trying to run across a freeway. The police had found a gun on the friend he was with at the time.

Just before his sixteenth birthday, we hired a psychologist to test him.

"Poor ego strength, poor academics, poor attention, poor impulse control, excessive suffering, excessive aggressiveness, and poor social conformity," the psychologist wrote in her evaluation.

Scott's writing was on a fourth-grade level—a trail of words sometimes scrawled in cursive, sometimes in print, with no indication of why he switched from one to the other.

"He stated that he would like to be a doctor when he grows up," she wrote. "He thinks he has the most trouble with schoolwork and would like to change himself so that he would be smarter."

Her diagnosis of Scott:

- Attention-deficit/hyperactivity disorder
- Adjustment disorder with mixed disturbance of emotions and conduct
- Developmental disorder of written expression

The psychologist recommended placing Scott in a remedial school and that he continue with counseling. She secured him a prescription for Ritalin—round little white pills prescribed to treat ADHD.

At first, he thrived on the drug, waking at 6 a.m. to focus on his schoolwork. But before long, he abused the medication.

I was still angry at John—so angry that I wrote him out of my first book.

"Jack, you cannot write about your life and leave John out," said a professor who read an early draft. "I don't know what happened between you two, but it would be disrespectful and dishonest."

So I found a few kind words to say and put him back in the story where he belonged. But I would not let him back in my heart.

In the fall of 1993, an old Young Life friend of mine called from Whitefish, Montana, to ask if I wanted to pastor the First Presbyterian Church of Whitefish, where he served as an elder.

I told him I wasn't interested, but then Leesa reminded me of several dreams she had over the last five years about us living in Whitefish.

I remembered the tiny town in the northwest corner of the state from when we vacationed there in the early 1980s. It was an outdoorsman's paradise.

I could not imagine living in a small town without an international airport. But by now, I had an immense respect for Leesa's dreams. She had dreamed about us moving to Anaheim to be with John Wimber when I had no desire to move there and instead thought I should start a church in Dallas. Before we ever left for Anaheim, she dreamed we would be there for four years and leave over a conflict.

Leesa was ready to go to Whitefish as soon as my friend extended the offer. I prayed about it for four months, and then we made plans to move to Whitefish.

I had no idea why God moved us to Whitefish, but I saw some immediate benefits. My Sunday morning stage was small, but the hunting was spectacular. I believed Scott would have a harder time finding freeways to cross and drugs to take in a town of three thousand people. That latter belief showed how little I knew about drugs.

———————

We moved into a house on the side of a mountain that overlooked a bright green meadow and a glacial lake that sparkled in the sunlight. Beyond them, one mountain after another rippled north all the way to Canada—jagged peaks that were home to bears, moose, deer, mountain lions, coyotes, and more bird species than you could name. From our deck, I watched golden eagles fly over the trees with squirrels clutched in their talons.

The church swelled in attendance from 170 to more than 300 in my first year as pastor. From a per-capita standpoint, we had become a megachurch. A tenth of the city turned out on Sunday morning.

People in the church said, "God brought you here to lead our church into revival."

I was surprised to find that not all members of the church felt the same way.

When four elderly women invited me for tea and cake one afternoon, I assumed they wanted to thank me. Instead they told me that all the new young people ruined their church. They hated the music. We sang half contemporary worship songs and half classic hymns. They wanted their hymns back—and nothing but their hymns.

"Ladies, I love the hymns too," I said. "But we have a lot of young people who love contemporary worship music. Should we just ignore the worship songs that are meaningful to them?"

"That music is not Presbyterian," they said. "Those young people are not Presbyterian. Some have only attended here for ten years. We've been here for more than forty years."

I tried to sympathize with their tiny frozen hearts.

Before we left for Montana, Mom had moved in with my sister, Debbie, and her physician husband just outside of town on a horse ranch. Bobbie, Mom's best and only friend, stayed at her side and came to "work" each day.

After we left for Whitefish, Mom lost interest in her grand-kids. I brought the boys from Montana to hunt doves in Texas in September 1995, but Mom did not care to see them. When Mom began wandering off from home, Debbie was forced to put her in a nursing home.

My brother Gary called me in Montana the next year.

"If you want to talk to Mom one last time," he said, "you better get back here quick. Her mind is going."

I did not go home.

A year after we relocated to Whitefish, I sat in my study praying when an unsought picture of me provoking John floated across my mind.

"Lord," I said, "was I really like that?"

A cascade of uglier scenes came and went. Over the next few days, I could not stop thinking about John. I picked up the phone.

"I'll be in California in a couple of weeks," I said. "Could we get together?"

"Sure," John said. "I'll be glad to see you, Jack."

John had limped into his sixties. Cancer. Stroke. Heart attack.

Carol answered their door and then walked me back to the kitchen, where John had parked his wheelchair in front of the breakfast table. The afternoon sun beamed through the glass patio doors, highlighting a person whose friendship had cost me my academic career. It was a small price to pay for the priceless education he had given me. His once-bulky cheeks had hollowed out a little, but his jovial expression was still intact. In his lap, he held a bucket for the unpredictable nausea with which he was consigned to live out his days.

"Well," I said, "it's been three years. Neither of us have said a negative word about the other."

"I know," he said. "We've been very disciplined in our bitterness."

My heart broke. No one could use humor to cut through the lies and go right to the heart of an issue like John.

"John, I came to ask you to forgive me, not just for the way I left, but for throwing away our friendship."

"But, Jack, I hurt—"

I raised my hand to cut him off.

"No, John, please don't say it. You would never have hurt me had I not repeatedly provoked you. A thousand young men would have given their right hands to be your right hand, but you picked me. I stand on stages around the world now. I've written a book that is selling all over the world. None of this would have happened without you being a father to me. I have been supremely ungrateful."

That was as far as I got before tears brought me to the ground at John's feet.

He put his right hand on my right shoulder.

"I forgive you, Jack," he said.

In stillness, I had sought God. He had visited me with a picture I did not want to see because it revealed so much ugliness in me. But in the discomfort of that light, gifts abounded. The strength to give up a grudge. The humility to ask for forgiveness. And the sensation of being loved—but not holy.

As I walked from John's house to my rental car I felt lighter, as though something evil had left me.

Thirty-Seven

R aised by a single mom over a bar in Wolf Point, Montana, Benny Bee grew up drinking and fighting. When his first marriage failed, his two boys went to live with him, and he taught them how to fight. He told them the secret to winning: "It doesn't hurt to get hit." He was short, but strong. When I first met him, he was trying to shed the thick layer of fat that encased his muscles.

Benny jumped out of bed every morning without an alarm at 4:30, and though he never attended college, he managed to acquire three radio stations in Montana. He had been a Christian for four years when we arrived in Whitefish. In church, I saw him cry during hymns and sermons.

We worked out every afternoon at the gym together. Others from our church joined us, even women in their sixties. Our children came too. It was our version of a healthy cocktail hour.

Benny's wife, Coco, a devout Christian who served on the city council, had beaten cancer five years earlier. One afternoon in the late summer, Leesa and Coco went hiking together at the local ski resort. Leesa returned downcast. Coco hadn't had a recent test. But Leesa said she knew, she just knew. The cancer was back.

Through no fault of his own, Benny was the spark that ignited a conflict in the congregation I had agreed to lead. A vacancy opened on the church's elder board, and I nominated him for it. Another

elder raised questions about his suitability for the job. She said
she heard from one of his employees that he managed his workers
harshly. I thought the criticism was unfair, and I told her so.

Benny wound up on the board. But the disagreement sowed
tremendous discord.

That year, I invited the Bees to a conference at a church in
North Carolina, along with our family. I wanted to have as many
people as possible lay hands on Coco and pray for her healing—
especially people who actually believed that God might heal her.
Scott went to the conference with us.

As Scott walked through the sanctuary after a meeting, he
caught the attention of a longtime Nashville studio musician. Don
Potter arranged music for the Judds. He was the leader of their
band and had coproduced their albums and written three or four of
their songs. He lived with his wife, Christine, in Adams, Tennessee,
northwest of Nashville, next to a Christian camp.

When he watched Scott pass by, he saw a younger version of
himself. Then he heard a voice say, *This boy is a time bomb, and
he will go off at the most inopportune moment.*

After the conference ended, Don invited Scott to his home.

It was the summer of 1995, and the popularity of grunge music
had begun to wane. Scott, however, was still immersed in it. But
the distorted, down-tuned riffs and angst-drenched lyrics of the
genre grated on the ears of one of country music's most celebrated
guitar players.

"How does it make you feel after you listen to it?" he asked Scott.

Trying to free Scott of bad influences, Don introduced him to
B. B. King, and Scott was mesmerized by King's fast-twitch vibrato
and liquid guitar string bends.

Scott told Don he had done pot, ecstasy, and other chemicals
Don had never heard of. He also revealed a deep-rooted inadequacy.

"I can never be a great man," Scott said. "My dad is great in
every way."

Scott confided that he wanted to kill the youth worker who had sexually assaulted him. How could someone he loved and trusted and looked up to as a spiritual leader betray him like that? But the confusion that the abuse created tormented him more than anything. Was he gay? Was he straight? How could he ever know?

That summer, I organized the whole church to fast and pray for Coco and anyone else who was sick. The first round of chemotherapy almost killed Coco. She refused a second round.

People said to me, "Now we know why God brought you here, Jack. So Coco can be healed."

I sat with Benny for hours in Coco's bedroom every day and prayed for God to heal her. Some days, Benny and I fell asleep on the floor beside her.

Coco kept right on dying.

In Tennessee, Don made Scott a counselor at the Christian camp adjacent to their farm. The kids loved him. Scott loved them back. He also loved a pet deer that the Potters kept, and he loved driving their John Deere tractor.

"Do you know the gospel?" Don asked Scott.

"Yeah, I know the words," Scott said.

They prayed together and cried together, and Scott asked Don to baptize him.

One evening, Don lowered my son's head into a river, and when he lifted him back up, Scott looked more peaceful and confident than ever.

Don wanted to ask Scott to live with Christine and him indefinitely. He knew Scott needed someone to walk with him.

But he worried that his offer might offend me. Who was he to offer such help to the son of a great man?

So Scott returned to Whitefish. He dated Cassie, Benny and Coco's daughter. Someone from the police force called Benny and said, "Your daughter rides around with that preacher's son, breaking every speed limit in town!" Benny laughed when he told me.

Don and Christine came to visit. Don brought his guitar. I took them over to the Bees, and the man who had played on more than a hundred number one hit records serenaded Coco with worship songs in her bedroom.

With her last strength, Coco raised her arms to God—offering him whatever she had left.

She stopped eating.

On September 15, 1995, Coco lay at home in a hospital bed surrounded by friends and family. She slipped into a coma. At 9:30, the death rattle gurgled in her throat. I kissed her good night, not good-bye. I planned to be back at dawn.

At 2:30 a.m., Coco's sister called.

"Jack, could you come over now?"

I could hear Benny weeping in the background.

When I pulled up, Benny was standing on the front porch waiting for me, crying.

"I never thought she would die," he said. "I never thought she would die. I never thought she would die, Jack."

I hugged him.

Then bounded up the stairs two at a time. It wasn't over yet. I held Coco's hand. It was still warm. But she wasn't breathing.

"Please, God. Please, God!"

It didn't work.

So I put my arms around her and commanded death to give Coco back. That didn't work either.

The darkness overpowered my faith. It paralyzed me. The

words I prayed dribbled out of my mouth, ran down my chin, and fell on the floor.

We had Coco's funeral on Monday. The whole town was there. Benny and I stood beside Coco's grave on a cold, overcast day. I said the last prayer, and then the rain fell.

I was empty of hope. I couldn't find any meaning in this story. All I could offer was a loving arm to put around Benny and the words, "Let's get out of here."

In the months that followed, I kept seeing Coco in her bed, arms stretched up to heaven.

What was more supernatural? A healing, or a heart that still worshiped as cancer ravaged the body in which it beat?

I could not say.

I just wanted a heart like that.

Thirty-Eight

Four months before Scott turned eighteen, he enrolled in Master's Commission, a full-time Christian discipleship school that churches all over the country hosted. Scott went to the school at the church in Kansas City founded by my friend Mike Bickle. The school created a structured environment for undisciplined and directionless young people stuck in that vast gray area between adolescence and adulthood. Volunteer host families from the church put up students from around the world. The school placed Scott and another boy named Mark with Doc and Nancy Fletcher. At first they shared a bedroom, but Scott's messiness exasperated Mark, so Doc and Nancy put the boys in separate bedrooms.

To the Fletchers, Scott seemed like a big Labrador puppy that bounced from person to person in search of a hug. While Mark tiptoed around the house, Scott bounded down the stairs with such force that he shook the pictures on the wall. Claiming that he was a germophobe, Scott refused to clean the church's toilets, a job other students did without complaint.

To teach them how to budget, the school limited the amount of cash students could receive each month, but I had given Scott a credit card in case of emergencies. Scott routinely used it to invite friends to lunch.

"How about we go out to lunch on Jack Deere?" he would say.

He made sure everyone knew I was his father, and when Doc

and Scott visited bookstores, Scott would find my books and create his own display on the bestseller table.

Whenever he made a mistake, Scott stuck out his thumb and forefinger in the shape of an "L" on his forehead and mouthed the word *loser*.

It was a side of him we never saw. To us, he could appear charming and confident, shiftless and defiant—but never self-loathing. And so we never saw that "L" on his forehead; instead we saw a big question mark.

Would he ever change? And if not, what then?

After two years in Whitefish, the conflict over Benny Bee joining the elder board ballooned into a war between the people who wanted to create a different church experience and those who clung to the past. A former member who had helped recruit me threatened to turn me in to the IRS, and soon after, I received a letter from the government that I had been selected for what proved to be a fruitless but time-consuming audit.

The vocal minority in the church launched a campaign with the regional presbytery to have me removed from the pulpit. Rather than fight that battle, I resigned. So did all the elders.

But I had no intention of leaving Whitefish. I had become close friends with perhaps the best bow hunter in the state, Terry Van Dyken. In the fall, I followed him on horseback into the mountains in search of elk.

At the end of a four-day hunting trip for elk or a day's hunt for deer, I spent happy evenings in Terry and Vanessa's small home, reliving our hunting exploits. I grew to love their three teenage sons, all of whom were excellent hunters.

The Van Dykens were one of the reasons that Montana had become a paradise for me.

On another dove-hunting trip to Texas, I finally decided to visit Mom in her rest home. It smelled of urine and decaying flesh, like the rest home I had worked in as a teenager. I found her shuffling down the hall, half moaning and half babbling.

"Hi, Mom."

She stared at me. Her eyes flickered with recognition that quickly disappeared. Someone had hacked off her hair. It looked awful. Maybe she had done it to herself. She was overweight and gray, and her cheeks sagged.

I took her hand and led her to Leesa, who threw her arms around Mom, but Mom didn't seem to know who Leesa was anymore.

I wanted her to sit down. But Mom wanted to lap the halls. So we walked. Leesa held Mom's hand and squeezed it. Mom smiled at her and squeezed back. Then an old woman shuffled by us, going the opposite way.

"She's a bitch," Mom said.

"Mom, don't talk like that," I scolded her.

"Well, she is a bitch."

"Mom, please."

Every person we passed was a bitch or worse. I told her to stop one too many times, and that scared her, and she disappeared into the shell that kept her on the earth.

Finally, she sat down on a sofa. I drew up a chair two feet opposite her. I looked into the eyes of the woman who made a fighter out of me and searched for any hint of her essence that might still linger in the body that used to be so beautiful. Maybe those grumbles and curses were all that was left inside.

We stared silently at each other for the longest time. Nothing. Tears rolled down my cheeks. I broke our silence.

"Mom, do you miss Dad?"

Her face turned sweet and sad. And her eyes looked into mine.

"Yes," she said.

"Me too," I said back.

And then she was gone.

Leesa and I did not speak in the car. I knew I had seen Mom for the last time.

I had waited too long to say good-bye.

At Doc and Nancy's house, Scott looked out the window every five minutes whenever any of us came to visit. When the doorbell rang, he ran to greet us. Doc expected to see an embrace. Instead, as soon as he opened the door, all the excitement drained out of Scott, and it seemed as though an eighteen-inch barrier had been placed between him and us.

As his graduation from Master's Commission neared, he was told to write how he had changed that year. He typed out a one-paragraph summary, with words randomly capitalized and sentences with misplaced punctuation.

"change comes slow," he wrote. *"change comes hard but change does come . . . This year, has been about dying to the Self, and choosing to do that every day."*

Perhaps he was sincere. But he also wrote a parody of the assignment to a friend as if he were addressing the students who would attend the school the next year.

Dear class of 96–97,

This is Scott Deere to tell you everything there is to know about Master's Commission. Firstly, don't drink and drive the first few weeks, this will get you into trouble. Also you need to heed the "don't murder while angry" ethic though you may be tempted to at times.

Enjoy a few beers but don't go too far. Most importantly, make sure to have some good excuses ready . . .

No ravaging of the girls is aloud—so cut it out!

That is all I have to say about that. Good-bye and good luck. Scott . . .

Scott came home to Whitefish ungrateful and surly. He slept in until noon and refused to work. I let it go on for a few months. But then I worried that by giving him free food and a free place to stay, I compounded the problem.

When I told him he needed to leave, Scott said he wanted to go back to Kansas City. I bought him a plane ticket and gave him $700 to get started. He talked Doc and Nancy into putting him up.

He worked at a Mexican restaurant and got in a car wreck with his coworkers, all of whom were high. Everyone suffered broken bones, except Scott. The restaurant fired him after it became clear he would always struggle with basic tasks, like remembering to refill water glasses.

He worked at a record store for a short time and then drove a street sweeper in mall parking lots at night.

Doc and Nancy learned about Scott's drug use and gave him an ultimatum.

"You can live with us," they said. "But you can't do drugs."

"Well, I guess I'm moving out," Scott said.

That October (1997), I appeared with John Wimber on a Christian TV show. He had to hold my arm for support as we stood in front of the camera.

A month later, an artery burst in his brain, killing him. Leesa and I flew to Anaheim. I was asked to write a tribute to John's life to be published after the funeral. I took out the hotel stationery, and tears poured out of my eyes, rivulets washing the words away. Leesa came up behind me and put her hand on my shoulder and said, "Oh, honey."

I could not stop crying. I could now see the beauty and greatness of God in the spiritual father I had spurned. But it took his death for me to realize it, and now I would never see him again.

Scott moved in with his aunt, Leesa's former sister-in-law, Penny, who lived in Kansas City with her two children. He lasted there a few months before he was asked to leave.

After that, he drove to Fort Worth, where he still had plenty of friends. But before long, Scott called me.

He said he was having a nervous breakdown and wanted to come home. If I would send him food and gas money, he would drive to Montana. I should have put him on a plane, for it was more likely that he was in withdrawal than suffering a nervous breakdown. Instead I sent him $300 through a friend in Fort Worth. Four hundred miles later, Scott wrecked his car.

He hadn't been arrested and his car was still drivable, but he was a basket case. I told him to drive to Colorado Springs, and I'd have another friend put him on a plane to Whitefish.

Scott arrived in Montana a few weeks before my speaking engagements in Portland and San Jose. I took him with me, along with Leesa and Alese. Being on his own had made him worse. He offended our hosts in Portland and terrified Alese, who locked herself in the bathroom of our hotel room. I didn't know what drugs he was taking, but he had to be taking something.

We checked into an expensive hotel in San Jose, and I called him to my room to talk to him alone.

"Scott, you have to leave and check into rehab," I said.

"I'm not going into rehab," he said.

"Then you just have to leave."

"Leave? What do you mean by leave?"

Thirty-Nine

I forbade Scott from having dinner with us that night. I told him to order room service if he wanted, but when we came back to the hotel room, he needed to be gone.

"Where will I sleep tonight?" he asked.

"I don't know."

"Dad, you're forcing me to sleep on the street."

"No, Scott, you're forcing yourself to sleep on the street."

"How can you kick me out?"

"You're killing everybody around you. I can't save you from yourself, but I can save them from you."

"I'm not going to rehab, Dad."

"Then it's time to say good-bye. I love you, Scott. I will miss you, and if anything happens to you, I may hate myself for the rest of my life. Good-bye."

"Good-bye, Dad."

But when we returned from dinner, Scott was still in our room.

"I'll go to rehab," he said.

The next morning, I learned that the most highly regarded rehab was Cityteam in downtown San Jose. There was a five-month waiting list. However, a close friend knew someone on the board and made a phone call that got Scott into the program within a week.

Scott settled into a routine and spoke well of the place, especially of the director, who had contracted malaria while he served as a missionary in Africa and couldn't wait to go back.

At the end of his first month at Cityteam, Scott met a lawyer's daughter in a convenience store. She picked him up in his free time and drove him around town in her BMW. Scott called me right about the time he completed his first sixty days in the program.

"My girlfriend rented a room for us in San Francisco for the weekend," he said. "Do you think it's okay if I go?"

"No, Scott, it's not okay," I said. "You're supposed to concentrate on getting and staying clean."

"I need a break."

"Cityteam won't give you permission to shack up with a girl for the weekend."

"They don't have to know."

"Scott, they are experts at detecting lies. They will find out, and they will kick you out."

"Okay, Dad."

I never found out if Scott took the girl up on her offer, but I don't think he was really asking for my advice. He wanted his dad to know that he still excelled at the one thing he had always been good at.

Or maybe he wanted to erase any doubts that he might be gay.

Although Scott often criticized the church for its hypocrisy and legalism, that never stopped people in the church from reaching out to him. I had close friends in the area—Dick and Carla Bernal, who pastored a large church in San Jose, and Rich and Wilma Marshall, who pastored a church in Sunnyvale. Dick's wife, Carla, picked Scott up at Cityteam and took him to church and to lunch afterward. Brian, one of the youth workers at the Sunnyvale church, visited Scott at Cityteam and took him to dinner and the movies.

At Cityteam, Scott had been given the task of manning the front desk, but he often charmed or fooled someone else into doing it for him. When that didn't work, he didn't show up. Once again, he depleted all his goodwill, and the other residents voted him out.

Scott spent Saturday night on the street. On Sunday morning, he loitered around the back of the Sunnyvale sanctuary. A woman named Nancy Duarte saw him, tapped her husband, Mark, on the arm, and said, "I don't know who that kid is. But he's special."

The couple was in their early thirties and owned a growing design firm.

The youth worker who took Scott to movies was Mark Duarte's brother-in-law. After the worship service was over, Brian asked Mark if Scott could stay at his house for the weekend.

"Yes," Mark said.

That weekend turned into a year.

Mark and Nancy weren't looking to adopt. Their daughter, Rachel, was fifteen. Their son, Anthony, was twelve. But in Scott, they saw the same thing that many others had: a lost boy who could become great if he could feel loved and find structure. They enrolled him in college, bought him a cell phone, and gave him his own room.

Night terrors visited Scott almost every night—dreams of people chasing him and trying to kill him. He told Mark he was terrified that he would die young.

In the evenings, Mark played the guitar and sang worship songs as Scott lay on the floor and stretched his hands toward heaven as if he were drowning and hoping to be rescued.

Scott got a job at Starbucks in downtown Mountain View, where he met his best friend, Sergio. When the line of customers stretched to the front door, Scott and Sergio became flamboyant speed baristas, tossing cups to each other, grinding beans, and pulling shots faster than anyone had ever seen. As the line dissipated, their audience burst into applause.

"Dad, two beautiful, young married women in their twenties who come into Starbucks every day asked me to sleep with them together. What do you think?"

"Scott, that is a crazy proposition. Don't do it."

"But, Dad, two women in bed with you—that's every guy's dream."

"It's not my dream. It could be your nightmare if their husbands come after you."

One night Scott thought the Duartes would be gone for the whole evening, and he invited a girl over. He was having sex with her on the diving board of the pool when he heard Mark and Nancy drive up. He shooed the girl out the back gate and ran into the house, wrapped in a towel. They figured Scott had gone for an evening swim.

In July 1998, the throat cancer that my hunting partner Terry had beaten five years earlier came back. I prayed and fasted for him. I took him and Vanessa to a conference so gifted healers could pray for him. I thought God would heal him. He was a great husband. He was the hero of his boys. He loved Jesus. But the cancer ignored the goodness of my friend and defied our prayers.

The tumor on the side of his larynx grew, crushing his voice box. Swallowing became difficult. Terry lost weight.

That fall, the mass had broken through the skin on his neck, oozing pus. He wore a bandanna around his throat as his mare carried him through the mountain forests.

As I rode behind him, the stench of his decaying throat floated on the wind.

In January 1999, Vanessa took Terry to a group of Christians in Connecticut to pray nonstop for his healing. She brought his body home in a white cardboard coffin.

I wasn't ready to give up. We placed the coffin in a small room and removed the lid. The plastic body bag was transparent. Terry wore the clothes he had died in. I could see his face. The plastic dulled his features. He looked like he was asleep. Then ten of us took turns gathering around the coffin, laying our hands on his body, and asking God to raise him up.

After a couple of hours of impotent praying, my faith ran out.

As I walked out of the room, I stared at a young widow and her three fatherless boys, and I wondered why my prayers were the most powerless for the people I loved the most. I silently vowed to look after Vanessa and her boys until it was clear that God had sent someone to take over Terry's role.

I presided over Terry's funeral service before a large crowd in Bozeman on February 7, 1999.

———

Scott made some A's at Foothill Community College in the fall of 1998, and the Duartes took not only Scott but Leesa and me as well to Maui for a week in February 1999. We ate lobster and steak and drank great Cabernets every night. We went whale watching and snorkeling during the day.

I swam beside Scott in the ocean fifteen feet below the surface to the turtles lying on the sandy bottom. A nearby sign read, "DON'T TOUCH THE TURTLES."

Scott swam to the biggest turtle, grabbed the back of his shell, and rode it all the way up to the surface.

I had not seen him this happy or grateful in the last ten years.

I was certain he was on the path toward recovery and that God had used the Duartes to save our son.

———

After a great year at the Duartes, Scott smoked pot again, used other drugs, and broke all the rules.

Rachel was confident and sassy like Nancy. She joked that she and Scott had a love-hate relationship: Scott loved her; she hated him. It was a joke. But she resented Scott for diverting so much of her parents' time and emotional energy to him.

Whenever Nancy confronted Scott, he argued with her and sometimes reduced her to tears. He took it for granted that she had rescued him off the streets and gave him his own room in her beautiful home.

After living with the Duartes for about eight months, he seemed to have realized he had crossed lines.

"I just wanted to check in with you and see if everything is okay between us," Scott wrote to Nancy in an email. "And lately you seem kind of mad at me still, or maybe just not interested. Or in other words, do you still love me?"

Of course Nancy still loved him, but she was also exhausted by him. At some point, Scott forced everyone who loved him to love him from a distance. The pain of being close to him was too intense.

"I'm not ignoring you, and, yes, I still love you," Nancy wrote back. "I just don't have much to say to you that's all. It's hard to have a conversation with you or in front of you because of the comments you make. So I limit my speech to only the necessities to avoid pain. As far as my love goes, that runs deep and true.

"Part of my pain is that I'm concerned, I solicit advice, I pray, I worry, I cry, and I'm tired. The responsibility of your life and success in many ways shifted to us somehow. We are praying long and hard about what the next phase of your life should entail."

She went on to complain that he had left food out in the kitchen, drove their truck when he wasn't supposed to, and stayed up so late that he often missed the classes they had paid for.

Mark called me to let me know that my son was putting him in a position of having to choose between Scott and his wife.

"Scott not only breaks the rules," Mark said, "but he disrespects Nancy. If he thinks I'll choose him over my wife, he's crazy."

When I called Scott to warn him, he said, "Dad, Mark would never ask me to leave."

But Mark did just that.

By mid-summer of 2000, Scott had run out of people to charm. He slept in a garage with a dog. I talked to Scott every couple of days, and he always told me how miserable it was sleeping in the garage. It killed me that my son was living like an animal, but I didn't tell him that.

Instead I said, "Scott, if you don't stop the drugs, that garage will seem like the Ritz Carlton compared to the next place you'll sleep."

I went to visit him in July. We stood in the parking lot of the Stanford Mall in Palo Alto.

"Scott, God really loves you," I said.

He looked down at the asphalt and muttered, "God loves everybody."

"No, Scott," I said, "you are really special to God."

"Everybody is special to God," he said.

I could offer Scott the knowledge of God, but not the experience of God, and knowledge alone could not penetrate the Kevlar vest of shame wrapped around his heart.

I sighed and gave up trying to convince him.

In the mid-1990s, I read an article about a Dell janitor retiring with nine million dollars' worth of stock. If a janitor could make that kind of money, couldn't I? I talked it over with Benny, and we both began studying the market, especially tech stocks that outperformed all the other stocks. We found a broker in town who had made millions. Benny was rich and had plenty to invest. I put all our savings into the market and borrowed more on margin to invest in a sure thing.

On some days, I made more than what was once my annual salary.

At our workouts, Benny and I had talked about God and the church. Now neither of us went to church, and the market's performance dominated our conversations. We not only bored but also irritated our weightlifting partners.

I wrote another book. It was about hearing God's voice. I traveled the world, speaking for God. And yet his importance in my life waned. I had more money than ever. I wasn't just smart anymore; I was rich too.

As Whitefish thawed in the spring of 2000, I drove down the mountain from my home to meet Benny at the gym. By summer, I could cash out of the market and never have to work again.

Then I heard the from-out-of-nowhere voice.

Sell everything, it said.

I knew it was God's voice. My voice would never have told me to sell everything. It made no sense to sell everything when each day my portfolio was growing in value. I should have listened. Instead I told myself that God surely didn't mean for me to sell everything right now.

Not until I had just a little more.

A few days later, the NASDAQ Composite Index peaked at 5,132 points. Then tech stocks plummeted. "Don't panic!" my investment advisers said. "It's only a small correction. It had to happen at some point."

I hoped they were right.

When I looked at my portfolio, I felt less rich and not so smart. By August, I was down almost 50 percent. I still had plenty of money—on paper. And the brokers still told me to be calm.

That same August, as I drove down my mountain, once again I heard the voice that would have made me rich if I had heeded it.

Bring Scott home, it said. *Treat him like the prodigal who has returned home. But know that he has not returned home.*

I'm so grateful that I listened.

———————

I hopped on a plane to Mountain View to rescue Scott from the garage.

"Scott, why don't you come back home to Whitefish with me for a few weeks, and we'll bow hunt for whitetail and elk, starting September 1?" I said.

He loved the idea. We had a great time climbing through the forests with bows slung over our shoulders, and in mid-September, I suggested that he move back to Montana.

"We can hunt all fall," I said. "I'll get you an apartment in Bozeman. I'll get you a car. You can go back to college at Montana State in January, and I'll pay your bills while you're in college."

"That sounds great, Dad," he said.

In the fall of 2000, I hunted all over Montana with my hunting partners—and I was the only father who brought his son on every trip. We climbed up mountains, hiked through fields, and traipsed through the snow in search of elk, antelope, deer, pheasants, and ducks.

I put Scott in an apartment with Terry's son Branden in Bozeman. I bought Scott a new four-wheel-drive Chevy Silverado pickup. He was accepted into Montana State for the next semester, beginning in January 2001. He got a job at a coffee shop in Bozeman and waited to restart college.

For the first time in twenty-two years, we didn't just talk; we communicated. One afternoon between hunting trips, I sat with him in our living room. He was on one side of the fireplace, and I was on the other. The two big elk mounts looked down on us from their place high above the mantel.

As the flames crackled, I remembered my violent reaction to Scott cursing his mom. The weight of what I had done seemed heavier than ever. I had never even asked him for forgiveness.

"Scott," I said, "you've heard me tell the story of how my dad showed me grace when I called my mom a damn shittin' rat."

"Dad," he said, "it's okay."

"It's not okay. You were only thirteen."

"Dad, it's okay."

"Scott, I have committed many sins in my life, and of all of them, that is the one I most wish I could take back. I failed you, Scott. If I could have just taken you by the hand and led you back to your mom to tell her you didn't mean it, she would have hugged you. Instead of bringing God's love to you, I brought shame and terror, and by the time I realized what I had done, you had already left home. I am so sorry. And I am so sorry that it's taken me all these years to apologize."

"Dad, I know. It's okay."

I couldn't tell if the apology meant anything to him or not.

In mid-December, Vanessa called to say she was worried that Scott was drinking too much. The police had found him at 4 a.m., passed out in his pickup. The windows were rolled down, and the temperature had approached zero. The newspaper published an item in its crime log but didn't mention Scott's name.

A psychiatrist in Bozeman had diagnosed him as bipolar and prescribed lithium for him. When he came home that Christmas, I didn't see any signs of depression. We talked about the upcoming school year and what he needed for his apartment.

One evening, Scott pulled into the driveway in his new pickup with a dented front bumper. He told me he hit a piece of furniture that had fallen off someone's trailer. I knew it was a lie.

We didn't find out until years later that two days before Christmas, Scott had driven out into the middle of a frozen lake.

He sat in his truck, waiting for the ice to crack.

Forty

On December 26, 2000, Scott drove south on Highway 90 to Kalispell with Alese to go to the movies. Snow and ice covered the road, but Scott pressed the accelerator to the floor. When the speedometer cracked 85 miles per hour, Alese wanted to caution Scott. But she recognized the clouds that settled in around him. If she spoke up, he would only have driven faster.

That night, he left with Benny's daughter, Cassie, around nine. I told him good-bye, not knowing when he might return home. I went to sleep upstairs around 11 p.m.

Sometime before dawn, a burst of noise jostled me out of a deep sleep. *What was that?* I listened for a few more seconds and then put my head back on the pillow.

I woke up at 7 a.m., made an espresso, and started a fire. I sank into the same chair in which I had apologized to Scott and worked on my next book.

Before long, Stephen woke up and went upstairs to my office to surf the internet. When he came to the kitchen for another cup of coffee, he asked if Alese was working out on the treadmill. He had heard a beeping sound from Scott's bedroom, where we had placed our treadmill.

I told him I would check.

When I opened the door, it took my mind a few seconds to un-scramble the details. There was my son, fully clothed, sitting on the floor with his back against the foot of the bed. Did he pass out before he could get into bed? Why was there glass on the floor? *Oh, no! Blood! He must have fallen and cut himself.*

Then the silver sheen of a gun barrel caught my eye. His right hand clutched my .44 Magnum revolver; his left hand still clung to a broken beer bottle.

"Scott!" His name emerged from my throat involuntarily, partly a wail, partly a plea.

He did not move.

I rushed to him, knelt beside him, and tossed the gun out of reach.

For a moment, I was alone with this awful knowledge. Soon I wouldn't be. And what then? How would his mother survive? How would I go on? I was at the border of a new world that was darker and more unforgiving than any other I had known.

I looked at the gun.

Use it, I heard a voice say. *It's the only way.*

Instead I stood up.

I shouted downstairs to Stephen. "Call 911! Scott shot himself!"

"What?" he yelled back, confused.

He raced toward Scott's room, and we passed each other on the stairs. Inside the room, Stephen picked up the gun and opened the cylinder, which contained only one shell case. Five unspent bullets lay between Scott's legs.

After calling 911, I returned to Scott's body.

"He was playing Russian roulette," Stephen said.

We could hear Alese moving around downstairs. Stephen went to find her to keep her from stumbling onto the scene cold. On his way out, he rammed his fist through the Sheetrock. He was furious at his brother.

Scott didn't just kill himself, he thought. *He probably just killed his father and mother.*

That's a hell of a way to punctuate all the pain he caused them.

I woke up Leesa. I told her what had happened.

"Please don't go in there," I said.

"If you don't let me go to Scott," she said, "I will never forgive you."

I put my white robe on her and led her to him.

We gathered around Scott's body. I held Scott's head, putting my hand over the exit wound so my wife wouldn't see it.

We asked God to bring him back from the dead.

Give him one more chance, please.

While we prayed, Leesa thought of all the other prayers she had prayed for Scott. *The joke's on you now,* she thought. *Some mother you turned out to be.* Demons danced on decades of pleas uttered for her second-born son—a boy deeply loved but now forever lost.

The police arrived and asked us to leave.

We headed downstairs, but then I looked at my hands. Leesa followed me back up to our bathroom.

As I ran my hands under the faucet, we stared wordlessly at the sink as Scott's blood, skin, and brain tissue disappeared down the drain.

Forty-One

As the police pieced together the last moments of his life, we called our closest Whitefish friends. Benny showed up within a few minutes. He threw his arms around me and cried.

He said Cassie had told him that Scott had bought drugs at a bar last night. She didn't know what the substance was. For the next few hours, Scott had faded in and out of consciousness. She had left him around 2 a.m.

Two other couples showed up to comfort us, and when the police left, the phone rang nonstop. Among the first to call were our oldest and best friends from Fort Worth, John and Nancy Snyder, who had helped us start Christ Chapel.

"Jackie, you come home right now," Nancy said. "You will stay with us. We'll take care of you."

Home.

I didn't know where that was anymore.

Our Montana dream home had become a house of horror. We could no longer stand to be there. We checked into a lodge a mile and a half down the road.

I didn't eat anything the whole day. That night, I took a bite of a sandwich and then threw it away. Eating was a betrayal of love. How could I enjoy food on the day my son had killed himself?

I tried to eat breakfast the next morning, but I could not tolerate the holiday laughter in the lodge's crowded restaurant.

Three days later, four seats opened up on a flight to Texas.

Back in Fort Worth, Nancy opened her front door and said, "You take that side; we'll take this side. And we'll grow old together."

Leesa crumpled into Nancy's arms.

Even though we were in a safe place, I could not make decisions. I let others pick out Scott's coffin and decide who would speak at his funeral.

At the service, the four preachers to whom I was closest spoke. But it was hardly a eulogy. Scott's friends from California hated what was said. They thought the speakers emphasized his dark side and ignored everything that made him so lovable.

The service ended with an invitation for Scott's nonbelieving friends to come down to the front to give their hearts to Jesus. I would have balked at giving an altar call at a funeral. Nevertheless, dozens of young people came forward.

Scott's best friend, Sergio, threw himself on the coffin. At that very moment, the sun broke through an opening in the overcast sky and sent a ray of sunlight through the round balcony window onto Sergio's head. He turned to look at the light, and his face and tears were radiant. The crowd gasped.

We buried Scott on January 2, 2001. As Leesa cried herself to sleep that night, she said, "I can't believe Scott is in the ground." I held on to her and said, "Honey, our bodies come from dust and then go to dust. We will see Scott again."

The next morning, on the front page of the metro section of the *Fort Worth Star-Telegram*, the headline read, "Dust to Dust." It was an article about the destruction of the sixty-seven-year-old Belknap viaduct on the eastern edge of downtown.

A few days later, a thunderstorm hit in the middle of the

night, and Leesa woke up, terrified that Scott was shivering in his coffin.

"Honey, he's not in the coffin. He's in heaven. He's praying for us right now."

"I know. I just don't want him to be cold. The ground is so cold and wet."

"But he's not in the ground."

"I know. It's just so cold. I can't help it."

The night that Nancy Duarte came home to California from Scott's funeral in Fort Worth, she dreamed she was sleeping and heard someone talking in her bathroom. Still in the dream, she got up out of bed and walked into the bathroom. Scott stood in the corner of the bathroom, talking on his cell phone.

"Yeah, I did that," she heard him say. "I have just one more thing to do, and I'll be there."

Nancy knew he was talking to God. Scott hung up. They walked to each other and hugged. Nancy could smell his musty smell—the nicotine mixed with his Calvin Klein cologne. Both of them cried, and he asked her to deliver a message.

"Tell Rachel that I know she loved me."

Then Nancy woke up.

That morning, Nancy sat with Rachel at the kitchen island. Rachel felt guilty for giving Scott such a hard time when he was alive. Nancy told her about the dream.

"It was so real that I could smell him and feel him," Nancy said. "It didn't feel like a dream. He told me to tell you that he knows you loved him."

Rachel broke down in tears.

While we were still at John and Nancy's, I received an email from
a reader. In one of my books, I wrote about my conviction that I
would be reunited with Dad in heaven. I don't think the man knew
about Scott's death. He just wanted to correct me.

"Suicides don't go to heaven," he wrote. "They can't confess
their last sin."

When the devil wants to send a message, he can always find a
religious person to deliver it with perfect timing.

But it didn't work. I had become a Christian thirty-five years
earlier, and at my moment of belief, the idea of Saint Peter's scales
was forever banished—at least as far as salvation was concerned.
Perhaps the only thing of which I was still certain was that no one
gains eternal life through good works. It is through faith in Jesus
alone. And once he is in our heart, he never leaves.

We can't possibly be aware of all our sins, let alone confess
them all.

———————

Scott's belongings arrived in a wardrobe box, the kind that movers
use when they pack up closets. Everything Scott owned fit in three
small duffel bags and one small box. When Leesa found some of
Scott's unwashed clothes, she put his black shirt to her face and
inhaled. I could smell the nicotine.

"Honey, I'll wash those clothes," I said.

"No!" she shouted. "I don't want to lose his smell."

I watched Leesa cling to the last physical scraps of her son on
earth, and I feared for our future.

She held on through her senses. I let go through my mind.

———————

I hated the amnesia of sleep. I woke up free for a few seconds each
morning and then learned I was in an endless nightmare. Although

I believed in a God who heals, I couldn't believe that my soul would ever be healed.

Once my life had a lofty purpose—to speak to churches and write books about God's goodness so that people would want a deeper relationship with Jesus Christ.

But Scott's death robbed me of the story I had told myself to make sense of my life. I had nowhere to go and nothing to do.

I still got out of bed at dawn. But I didn't know why.

A couple of weeks after the funeral, someone suggested we go out for an evening. I didn't want to, but I told my family that I thought maybe we should.

We had almost made it through dinner when Leesa broke down. She was so sorry, she said. She didn't want to spoil things. She would try to sit through the movie, but nobody wanted to watch a movie, so we headed home.

I stopped at a convenience store. I saw an old friend flipping through the magazines. He had recently lost his wife, Deborah, to colon cancer. He told me he was writing a book about his life with her. He wasn't a writer; he was an art dealer. I thought the book would go nowhere. The book—*Same Kind of Different as Me*—would make the *New York Times* bestseller list and become a movie with A-list stars.

As Ron and I talked for a few minutes, I noticed that the mischievous sparkle had left his eyes. His voice was flat. He talked about death in the analytical tones of a medical examiner.

He came out to the car to say hi to my family. He took one look at Leesa and said, "You all are not even out of shock yet."

Later that night, Leesa told me she couldn't go on. All she ever wanted to be was a wife and mother. Now twenty-two years of prayers and mothering had disappeared with the pull of a trigger. I pointed out how much joy Stephen and Alese had given us.

"We still have them," I said.

Her despair lifted momentarily.

Then she said that Stephen and Alese had turned out good in spite of her.

Hurling logic at Leesa's shame turned out to be as helpful as throwing rocks at the devil.

Still, I tried to save Leesa by becoming a student of her grief. I took notes every day about anything—a song, a smell, a sight— that triggered a memory that turned into tears, like when in the supermarket one day, she saw a young boy Scott's height and build with a baseball cap turned backward.

Two weeks after we buried him, the funeral bill arrived. It was $10,064.69. Thirty minutes later, my secretary walked in the room with a sack of mail. I dumped out thirty-eight sympathy cards and letters, which contained twenty-two checks—one for each year of Scott's life.

I added them up. The total: $10,065.00, a few pennies above the cost of putting his body in the ground. I was stunned. I didn't need the money. I still had plenty in the bank to pay for Scott's funeral.

"What are you saying, God?" I asked.

The voice of mercy, the voice I had ignored for money, spoke to me through money. It said, *I paid for his death. I also paid for his life. And I'll pay for everything you ever need for as long as you live.*

That February, a church in Amarillo, Texas, that I spoke at once a month needed me to introduce a special speaker at their weekend services because all their senior pastors were out of town. So I left Leesa in the care of Stephen and Alese for twenty-four hours. It was my first time in a church service since I had lost Scott eight weeks earlier.

After the first service ended, I stood at the front of the church with the prayer team. I spotted someone moving toward me. I couldn't tell if the person was a man or woman, a girl or boy. The person did not have a face. Where the mouth should have been was a misshapen hole, and what once was a nose was no longer recognizable as a nose. The blind eyes were slits sealed shut. A plastic tube protruded from a hole in the throat, a permanent tracheostomy.

An attractive blonde woman led the person by the arm.

"Hi, I'm Michelle," she said. "This is my son Aaron. Six months ago, Aaron was so distraught that he put a shotgun under his chin and pulled the trigger. The blast blew away his face. It has taken multiple surgeries to get him to this place. He doesn't believe in God, but he came down here with me because I asked him to. Would you pray for Aaron?"

The last time I laid hands on a person in prayer was when I held Scott's head and asked God to bring him back from the dead.

"Aaron, my name is Jack," I said. "Would you like me to pray for you?"

He put his finger over the tube to keep the air from escaping before it could go through his vocal folds and said, "Yes."

I put my right hand on his back. When my left hand touched his heart, power fell on me. It rippled down my neck, down my back, down my legs. I knew what to pray.

"Aaron," I said, "my twenty-two-year-old son Scott pulled the trigger at Christmas, but he didn't make it. God spared your life because he still has purposes for you, if you want to fulfill them."

"I'm so sorry," said Michelle. "I didn't know. I heard about the minister whose son . . . whose son . . . I didn't know it was you. I'm just so sorry. I would never have brought my son to you if—"

"Michelle, don't be sorry. You haven't done anything wrong. I'm glad you came to me. I'm glad to pray for Aaron. God made this appointment between us," I said.

I finished praying for Aaron. Then I prayed for Michelle and felt the same power descend on me.

After they walked away, I couldn't tell who had benefited more from the encounter—Aaron or me. I looked up and offered a silent, spontaneous prayer.

"Man!" I said, "You are really something!"

God was strengthening me in the most broken places and teaching me to embrace a mystery as if it were a friend.

Forty-Two

B efore Scott's death, I sometimes flew 160,000 miles a year to speak at conferences all over the world. Leesa quit flying with me. She wanted to stay home and enjoy her friends, or at least that's what she said. While Scott bounced from one benefactor to another, Stephen was away at college, earning his journalism degree. Alese, then sixteen, was at home with her mom.

In May 2000, I noticed the first clear signs of a destructive pattern in Leesa's drinking.

Leesa and I left a three-hour dinner with wine-drinking friends, and on the way to the car, Leesa grabbed my hand to steady herself.

A couple of times in the fall, the sound of Leesa falling down awakened me in the middle of the night. I found her passed out on the bathroom floor.

She weighed seventy pounds less than me, but still drank the same amount. We drank every night. Deep down, I knew she had a problem. I also knew I had one. But I didn't confront her about it, perhaps because doing so would have forced me to admit that I drank too much wine.

Then Scott died.

After six weeks with John and Nancy, we moved into a rented house. A van brought our furniture and hundreds of bottles of wine from my wine cellar.

Leesa cried herself to sleep nearly every night. Every afternoon, she opened her first bottle of wine before she cooked the evening meal.

Over the next few months, I lost the rest of my stock market money, and we lived off credit. I earned no money until I went back on the conference circuit in 2002. That summer, as I took my seat on an American Airlines 737, leaving Orange County, California, my cell phone rang.

It was Leesa.

"Honey, I've got some bad news for you," she said. "Your mom died this morning."

We buried her at Rose Hill Cemetery on the east side of Fort Worth. Bobbie and her son Pete came. Bruce and Phillip also came.

I stood behind the little lectern at the funeral home and felt fake. I had seen Mom the least in the last eight years. I couldn't say anything about her that everyone in the room didn't already know. But I was the preacher. Everyone expected me to talk.

I took five minutes to say that Mom was a saint. I still partly believed it.

Then we rode up the hill and put Mom's coffin in the ground next to Dad's.

I had become close friends with B. J. Weber, one of the chaplains for the New York Yankees, and often stayed in the basement of his Manhattan brownstone. In December 2002, he told me about a former Goldman Sachs partner who had started a men's ministry.

"Why don't I cook steaks and get my friend Jim to come over for dinner with us tonight?" B.J. asked. "We'll drink some great wine."

"Sounds fine to me."

That evening, the door burst open. In walked Jim Lane.

"Hey," he yelled, throwing his arms around me and slapping me on the back as if we'd been friends forever.

"So I hear you're a wine lover," Jim said. "What's your favorite?"

I told him. That wine was so rare that I had never seen it in a wine store, only on the wine lists of exclusive restaurants in California.

"Come to my house and speak to my men's group," he said. "I'll give you a bottle."

He was fifty-one, three years younger than me. His hair had turned gray, but he retained the athletic build and ruddy looks of his youth. Blueblood ran through his five-foot-eight-inch frame and mingled with evangelical nobility. When Billy Graham attended Wheaton College, Jim's grandparents directed Graham's spiritual life.

Goldman Sachs crowned Jim a partner when he was still in his early thirties. But life as a multimillionaire left him empty. He began to drink too much and cheated on his wife. The shame took its toll.

In the early eighties, Jim met B.J., who cared for street people in Manhattan.

Jim wanted to confess what he had done, but didn't know how B.J. would respond.

"I have this friend who . . .," he told B.J. over lunch.

B.J. did not act surprised. He did not condemn. He didn't offer clichés. He sympathized with the anonymous sufferer. Little by little, Jim revealed that the friend was him.

That confession helped Jim find God's forgiveness. It also made him realize he could not pursue God on his own. Like many other men, he didn't care for the traditional church services that featured forty-five-minute sermons about everything he ought to be doing. So instead he invited seven men to come to his house for breakfast on Friday mornings.

I pulled up to Jim's snow-covered, five-acre estate in New

Canaan, Connecticut, in February 2003. Jim hugged me as I walked through the front door.

"Come into the kitchen," he said. "Get some coffee and breakfast."

Jim's caterer had prepared his own version of the Egg McMuffin, which sat next to mounds of pastries, preserves, butter, fresh fruit, and urns of gourmet coffee.

Jim shook hands with the new guys and slapped the old guys on the back. Some wore tailored suits and expensive Italian ties. But others had on jeans and down vests and work boots.

Soon the place was noisier than a Friday happy hour, but I could hear Jim's distinctive, loud, high-pitched laugh two rooms away.

At 7 a.m., Jim walked through the house and yelled, "Time to start."

The seven men had turned into a crowd of 150 squeezed into a living room dismantled to accommodate them.

A four-piece band—keyboard, drums, and two guitars—sat up on its stage next to the fireplace and played worship songs. Then Eric Metaxas, a comedian and bestselling author, made announcements that served as a pretext for his jokes.

"I want to welcome all the new guys this morning," he said. "In spite of what you may have heard, we are not a cult. However, the mother ship will be here at nine o'clock to take us home to our real planet if you want to go."

"We've looked forward to this meeting for a long time because we lined up a famous speaker who needs no introduction. Unfortunately, that speaker cancelled on us at the last minute.

"But we were able to replace him with another speaker who needs no introduction. Unfortunately, he also cancelled.

"Unfortunately, the itinerary of everyone we asked to take his place was full.

"Finally, we found a speaker whose itinerary was open, exceptionally open.

"Our speaker this morning does require an introduction.

"He's from Texas."

Eric frowned and shrugged.

"I know. I know. I apologize. But I told you, we were in a pinch.

"His academic résumé isn't really very impressive, so I won't embarrass him by mentioning it. He has written some books, which I'm sure none of you have or will read. So I won't take time to mention them either.

"I will mention one outstanding achievement. He was a professor at Dallas Theological Seminary. For those of you who don't know, Dallas Seminary is a small fundamentalist graduate school somewhere in the South. Maybe Dallas, but I'm not sure.

"Our speaker had an emotional breakdown and joined a cult in Southern California, and the seminary fired him."

Then Eric said a few endearing things about me, but not a lot.

I stood up to speak amid applause and feigned jeers and waited for them to quiet down.

"Eric," I said, "thank you for the introduction. You must know how intimidating it is for a Texan to speak to all these educated people. Even you, who graduated from Yale—a fact you were happy to share with me in the first five minutes of our meeting.

"I know that some of the kind, discerning, intelligent, and truly Christian men in the room may have thought your humor was a bit harsh. And maybe it was, but I want you to know from the bottom of my soul that when someone treats me harshly or mocks me, it is my policy to simply overlook it.

"I would never draw public attention to the thoughtless use of sarcastic, highbrow humor by a pseudo-intellectual from an Ivy League school, all at my expense.

"I'm sure you are a decent man. And some day, they will discover a therapy or a medication that will prove me right."

The room filled with applause and laughter. Eric himself roared.

"Hey, Eric," someone yelled, "how does it feel to finally get some payback?"

Then I opened my Bible and talked for the next twenty-five minutes about how loving Jesus is the greatest experience in the world.

It was just like a Young Life club for middle-aged men, many of whom were wealthy.

It felt like home.

Forty-Three

In Fort Worth, I had rebuffed invitations to become the pastor of a church I spoke at regularly on Sunday mornings. It was called New Church, had about 250 people, and was located in a suburb northeast of Fort Worth.

My desire to build the "super church" had resurfaced. New Church seemed to provide the best opportunity for my vision. I took the offer.

I renamed the church Wellspring and expected crowds to appear. They did not. I hadn't experienced that kind of failure since my first days of leading a Young Life club. Each Sunday, I returned to the stage with that same resilience. But empty chairs chipped away at my pride.

I prayed for the church to grow. And then I prayed some more. I thought that God was testing me.

I didn't consider that church wasn't about me or that instead of asking God to bless my church, I should have asked how my church could bless God.

While only 250 people showed up to hear me speak at Wellspring on a Sunday, thousands gathered at the conferences where I spoke.

On a trip to Cape Town, South Africa, in 2004, Leesa disappeared into the airport lounge, only to return tipsy. When we settled into our hotel room, she asked for wine at lunch.

I told her no, and we fought over that glass of wine for most of the afternoon. We showed up to dinner with my admin, Aaron, angry at one another. At first, we tossed lighthearted barbs at each other, eliciting laughter from Aaron. But the wine made me mean as I reminisced about other trips.

"Honey, remember the vacation in the Philippines," I said, "when the raw fish you had at dinner made you sick? The hotel doctor gave you medicine, but you refused to take it because he was just a hotel doctor. So you spent the next two days in bed, and when we landed in LA, we had to rush you to the emergency room so the doctors who spoke English with an American accent could offer you the exact same diagnosis and the exact same medicine.

"Only they charged us thousands of dollars for the medicine and the IVs to cure your dehydration."

Aaron stopped laughing when he saw the humiliation on Leesa's face. Leesa left the table and stormed down the hall toward our room. I followed her. She wondered out loud if her life would have been better had she married her high school sweetheart.

When I came out of the bathroom, Leesa said, "I'll see you in heaven."

"What have you done?"

"Nothing. I'll see you in heaven."

"Have you taken something?"

When she didn't answer, I rushed back into the bathroom and found an empty bottle of sleeping pills. I called the manager, who called for an ambulance.

At the hospital, Leesa was groggy and incoherent. The doctors drew blood, decided not to pump her stomach, and then put in IVs. When she came to, she wept and said over and over, "My son shot himself, and my husband hates me."

I tried to tell Leesa that I loved her and that I was sorry, but she never heard me. Finally she went to sleep, and I went back to the hotel at 6 a.m.

Three hours later, I dragged myself onto a stage. I told 1,500 people how to hear the voice of God and received a standing ovation.

Almost as soon as I stepped away from the stage, the confusion, pain, and terror broke out of the vault I had shoved it in while I spoke to the crowd. I returned to Leesa in the ICU. Her hair was tangled and soaked in sweat, and I bent down to embrace her.

"Honey, I am so sorry for being so cruel to you last night," I said.

"I'm sorry I put you through all this," she said. "I don't know what happened. I just lost my mind."

I persuaded the doctor to release Leesa instead of requiring a stay in the psych ward, which was normal hospital protocol.

At the hotel that same day, Leesa again asked for a drink at lunch.

A few weeks later, at about two in the afternoon, I opened our bedroom door to see Leesa with a glass of wine.

"I'm losing every bit of affection I have for you," I yelled at her. "Stop drinking in the daytime! Stop drinking behind my back!"

I headed to the gym to rid myself of rage. In the middle of a bench press, I envisioned her swallowing more sleeping pills. I ran out of the gym and drove home to find her sitting in our bedroom as though we'd never had a fight.

"Honey, I'm sorry I screamed at you," I said.

"It's okay. I know I scared you."

"I'm going to stop drinking," I said. "I want you to stop drinking too."

"I'll stop drinking for you."

"That won't work. You have to stop for yourself."

"Okay, I'll stop."

I put a lock on the wine cellar door and stopped drinking.

In November 2004, two hundred men showed up at Jim Lane's New Canaan estate for the Friday morning meeting. But Jim was nowhere to be found. A couple of the guys went upstairs to look for him. His bedroom door was locked.

"Go away," yelled Jim.

"We're not going away," they said.

After a few minutes, a red-eyed, unshaven, hungover Jim opened the door.

"I want to die," he said.

"That's not an option," said one of the men.

"We're all in this together," said another. "Together we'll figure a way out." He'd been on a two-day binge.

They talked for hours. The encounter ended with Jim's surrender.

"I'll do whatever you say," he said. "I'm so sorry."

They reserved a room for him at a rehab in Minnesota.

Jim did his twenty-eight days and returned home determined to stay sober. Everyone in Jim's Friday morning group—dubbed the New Canaan Society—knew where Jim had been. Had he been the pastor of a church, the board would have fired him. They might have paid for his rehab, but he would have been sent to a new congregation, maybe in another state.

But this was not church. This was a few hundred businessmen striving to love Jesus and each other.

Jim feared that his rehab stay would destroy the Friday morning meetings, but three hundred men—the largest NCS crowd ever—embraced their sober, alcoholic leader with a standing ovation on his first Friday morning back.

Forty-Four

In the fall of 2004, both Stephen and Alese were home for the weekend, when I again confronted Leesa for the hundredth time about her drinking.

"I'm just not ready to stop," she told me.

She collapsed in an inebriated heap on the bathroom floor. I brought the kids in, who were now both in their twenties. We implored her for an hour and a half. She insisted she could control her drinking if I would just let up on the pressure.

"Is that so?" I asked. "Then why did you try to kill yourself in Cape Town by swallowing all those sleeping pills?"

It was the first time our children had heard about her attempted suicide.

Leesa screamed at me and took a harmless swing.

"You need to go to rehab," I said.

"I'm not going to rehab."

"Why not?" I asked.

"I'm just not," Leesa said. "I'll stop drinking now."

We concluded the impromptu intervention with the agreement that if Leesa had one more drink, she would have to start AA or rehab, whichever I chose.

_____

The first step of Alcoholics Anonymous's twelve steps says, "We admitted we were powerless over alcohol—that our lives had become unmanageable."

It's also the first step for members of Al-Anon, the support group for the loved ones of alcoholics.

I pushed Leesa toward AA, thinking it was the way she would sober up. I wanted her to admit she was powerless, but I was unwilling to admit that I, too, was powerless over her drinking.

I remained confident that, one way or another, I could get her to put down the bottle.

The second step in AA and Al-Anon says, "Came to believe that a Power greater than ourselves could restore us to sanity." But to do that, you have to acknowledge that your life is insane—a step I didn't know I needed to take.

I saw myself as the enduring husband willing to go to any length to save his wife, and yet my ignorance and arrogance were robbing her of her dignity.

I had told my wife that she had to choose sobriety for herself and then tried to force her to make that choice.

I had treated her like a child and then expected her to make decisions like an adult.

———

In January 2005, we flew to Minneapolis and rented a car for the hour-and-a-half drive north to Center City so Leesa could spend twenty-eight days in rehab at Hazelden—the same program Jim had completed.

At the intake desk, Leesa wept. The counselor asked Leesa some questions about her drinking. Leesa told her that a couple of weeks ago, she had wandered out of the house in the dead cold of the night in a nightgown and barefoot.

"If you do that here, you'll freeze to death before we can find you," she said.

I stayed the first week and did the family program. At the end of Leesa's first week, I flew home on Saturday. I had visions of her walking out into the subzero Minnesota night. I saw myself standing in the Minneapolis airport, watching her body travel up the conveyor belt in a white cardboard coffin.

She called me crying for the first few days after I left, and then she calmed down and accepted her fate.

Leesa loved meeting with her primary group of eight women. Under the guidance of a recovered alcoholic, each member of the group told her story to the group. Their meetings were miniature AA meetings. After a couple of weeks, she said to me over the phone, "I wish church could be more like AA."

"What do you mean?"

"Well, everyone here is so honest, and no one condemns anyone."

———

A day after I brought Leesa home from Hazelden, she went out for lunch and didn't return home. At 5 p.m., I began calling her cell phone. No answer. At 6 p.m., she answered.

"Jack?"

"Where are you?"

"On a freeway."

"What freeway?"

"I don't know."

"Pull off the road, now!"

"I don't want to come home."

"You have to pull off the road before you get into a wreck."

"I don't want to live."

"Please pull off the road now."

"Oh no, there's a cop behind me."

"Leesa, pull off the road or you're going to jail."

"Okay. I'm parked."

"Where are you? I'll come get you."

"I don't know."

"What street are you on?"

"I don't see a street sign."

"What do you see?"

"A fence and airplanes."

"Okay. Just stay there, and I'll find you."

The Dallas Fort Worth airport is huge, covering more than 18,000 acres, a larger landmass than Manhattan. I drove down roads I had never been on to a section outside the airport I'd never seen. And I saw our black Suburban on the side of the road. Inside, Leesa had passed out.

When we got home, I carried Leesa to bed. She was comatose. Worried that her body was shutting down, I called 911. The paramedics took her to the hospital. Her blood alcohol concentration (BAC) was .388. A BAC of .4 can be fatal.

When she woke up the next morning, she said, "I lost my mind. I will never drink again. Please forgive me."

I studied alcoholism even more than I studied grief. If I could understand how the disease worked, I could halt its progress in Leesa, whom I saw less as a person to be loved than as a problem to be fixed.

As my knowledge grew, I gave a series of talks about alcoholism at a Wednesday evening class at Wellspring. One was about detaching from "your alcoholic." I told people that allowing your well-being to rise and fall on the sobriety of a loved one will only make you miserable. But that was exactly what I was doing.

Some people in the church knew that Leesa had spent time in rehab. I'm sure they assumed I spoke from personal experience.

Leesa, who sat in the front row, was humiliated.

I was oblivious.

In July 2006, Leesa traveled with Stephen to help him move into his new loft in St. Louis, where he had taken a job as a reporter for the *St. Louis Post-Dispatch*.

That weekend, Alex, an old friend, came to Fort Worth to preach at my church. He brought along his wife, Mary. It had been years since I had seen them.

At 6:30 on Sunday morning, Mary and I sat at our kitchen island drinking coffee. She confided in me that her father had sexually abused her as a teenager. A few years ago, she had taken Alex with her to confront her father, who broke down, admitted what he had done, and apologized.

In the twenty years I had known her, it was the first serious conversation we had ever had.

"I always thought you were afraid of me," I said.

"I was afraid of you," she said. "I was afraid of all men."

But the confrontation with her father gave her courage she had never thought possible. She went back to work and built a successful company on her own.

A photograph of Leesa from when she was in second grade had vexed me for years. In the black-and-white picture, bags appear under her eyes. What child has bags under her eyes?

After Alex and Mary left, Leesa and I spent a week alone at a farm in the hills of Dorset, Vermont.

"You'll never believe what happened to Mary," I said.

As I told her Mary's story, she could hear the admiration in my voice. A few nights later, we lay in bed. Leesa confessed that for seven years of her childhood, her father had regularly sneaked into her bedroom and sexually assaulted her.

What she remembered most about grade school was her teachers' rebukes for falling asleep in class after her dad had kept her up at night.

The bags I saw in the picture held the secret to her shame.

After thirty-two years of marriage, I had only begun to understand my wife.

Forty-Five

On Saturdays, while her mother was at work and her two brothers played outside, Leesa's father forced her into sex acts before she could go outside.

Leesa remembered one night, when her mother walked in while her father was abusing her.

"Oh, Tommy!" she cried.

"Get out!" the coach yelled.

She did.

By the time she was twelve, Leesa had enough. When he tried to join her in the shower, she screamed at him. He never tried anything after that.

"I'm not good," she had said in the moonlight by the lake when she was nineteen years old. Thirty-three years later, I finally understood what she meant. In her mind, she never had any sexual purity to protect, only her shame to conceal.

It made sense now. What didn't make sense was why she had never told me.

She said, "I didn't think you would want me if you knew what I had done."

What she *had done?*

After all these years, she still thought of herself as a coconspirator, not as a victim. That is part of the power an abuser has over a child. Leesa told me some of the unprintable details, as much as she thought I could tolerate.

Now I understood why Leesa was often quiet in social settings. She would walk into a room full of people who were talking and laughing and think, *If these people knew who I really am, they wouldn't want me in this room.*

While I had once been confident I could stop her drinking, I had no idea how to repair a soul bludgeoned by years of secret shame. I finally asked for help and learned about a rehab center in Arizona. They treated not only addictions, but also childhood trauma that leads to adult dysfunctions.

Leesa was there for four weeks before Alese and I joined her for family week.

When I saw Leesa for the first time in twenty-five days, she looked a decade younger. On the way to our first lecture, we cut through a sea of sweet smiles and floated on arias of "Hi, Leesa," "Hey, Leesa," "How ya doin', Leesa?" She had become the queen of the rehab. For the first time, I was in her shadow.

"Jack, this will be a hard week," she said.

"Don't worry, honey," I said. "We'll all be fine."

But she knew better.

From the beginning, one rule was made clear. We weren't to talk about personal or family issues unless we were in the presence of counselors. We paid for their guidance to resolve issues we couldn't resolve on our own. If we talked about those issues, we risked undoing their work or stymieing it.

I violated the rule at our first lunch. Leesa and Alese refused to engage. So we ate in silence.

In a session the next day, a counselor asked me, "Do you always interact like this?"

"Like what?"

"Like that," he said.

"I have no idea what you mean."

"Your tone, volume, and expression are all angry."

He seemed to be insinuating that I was part of Leesa's problem. I didn't appreciate it. I was the victim, not the perpetrator.

By the second night, my daughter stopped speaking to me.

We met with Leesa's primary therapy group of seven other residents each day. She loved them. I couldn't stand them.

"Jack, when you speak, I hear my father's voice," said a twenty-seven-year-old man named Bobby. I didn't know his story, but I knew that what he said to me was not a compliment.

The group let out a collective sigh.

I wanted to say, "Maybe you should have listened to your father's voice, and then you wouldn't have become a chronic relapser."

Instead I said, "Thank you, Bobby."

At a meeting near the end of the week, I looked around the room and realized that everyone had sat in a specific place. Leesa sat in front of me with Alese and two counselors. Her primary group was to the left in a semicircle.

The meeting was a setup.

"Leesa would like to tell you how your anger has hurt her," one of the counselors said. "Would you like to hear it?"

It wasn't much of a choice.

"Yes," I said.

"Okay," she said. "You may respond in three ways. You may agree. You may disagree. Or you may ask for more information.

You cannot argue, justify, excuse, or accuse. This is a time for you to listen. Do you understand the rules?"

"Yes."

Leesa took out a list.

She rattled off the story of her humiliation in church when I talked about detaching from "your alcoholic." She couldn't understand how I could be so callous. I was embarrassed at my own insensitivity.

"Would you like to respond?" her counselor asked.

"It's true," I said. "I'm sorry."

And so it went—story after story.

Finally, the counselor said, "I think that's enough, Leesa."

All I could do was listen and feel sad.

The next day, I asked a counselor, "Do you think I could benefit from a week in your trauma program?"

The counselor was the one who had diagnosed me as an angry person. Their trauma program offers group therapy that deals with the trauma of a person's early life.

"I've already taken the liberty of reserving you a place next Monday morning," he said.

Forty-Six

The group therapist asked me to draw a picture from childhood and then to explain it. I took a black marker to butcher paper and drew stick figures: a table with a tiny boy under it, two smaller boys standing in the doorway to the kitchen, and Mom five times larger than anyone else. The flyswatter she held in her right hand was twice as large as me. I drew long wires in every direction for her hair.

I hung the picture on a blackboard and told the "f-word" story with my back to the group. Usually it made people laugh.

When I turned around, four women had tears in their eyes. The other man in the group shook his head.

"I thought that was funny," I said.

"Look at the picture a little more closely," said the therapist. "What's the little boy doing under the table?"

"He's hiding."

"It's more like cringing, isn't it? Why is he hiding from his mother?"

"He's terrified."

"Look at your mother in proportion to you. You made her five times larger. What's that saying?"

"Maybe it's impossible for the little boy to defend himself."

"Now tell us again: What's funny about that picture?"

I couldn't respond.

At this rehab center, they wouldn't allow me to heal myself by turning my beatings into acts of hilarity.

The six of us in my therapy group were together for a reason: We were the products of traumatic childhoods with abusive mothers and passive fathers. For the next few days, I listened as members of my group struggled to draw connections between their upbringings and their adult dysfunctions. Everyone in the group could make those connections easily—for other people.

The therapist had forbidden any of us to give advice. She knew we had to discover the connections for ourselves in order to change. So she plied us with leading questions. Sometimes it worked; sometimes it didn't.

"Everything we experience passes through a filter in our minds so we can make sense out of our lives," she said. "Sometimes that filter gets covered with crap in our childhood, and we grow up believing lies about ourselves and about other people. Sometimes our filters tell us lies that protect our destructive behavior. This week is about cleaning that filter."

At the end of the week came "the experiential"—an exercise to release years of anger that have imprisoned our hearts. The day before, I wrote a letter to Mom, Dad, and Poppa, my maternal grandfather, saying things to them that I'd never had the chance to say while they were alive.

The therapist turned the lights off and closed the blinds. I sat at the end of the room with the window at my back. The therapist sat in front of me. The rest of the group sat against the wall to my left. The therapist told me to close my eyes and leave them closed for the duration of the session.

"I want you to think of a pleasant time when you were fifty-two," she said. Then she asked what I saw. I told her I was in my home on a Montana mountain, serving Silver Oak wine to our friends.

Then she walked me backward through my history, pausing at what seemed to be random increments of my life, to sample what was going on at different ages.

"I want you to think of a peaceful time in your childhood," she said. "Picture the house where you lived."

I remembered the front yard of our Yeager Street house and my favorite photo, the one when I was six years old, standing with my two younger brothers dressed in our Davy Crockett outfits and holding Jungle Jim rifles.

I looked at that little boy in the center.

He is a good kid. He loves his mama and daddy. He is sweet. He is happy. And he has no idea of what is coming.

"Is there anything you would like to say to that little boy?" the therapist asked.

I wanted to hold him.

"Jackie, everything will be all right," I said. "God will rescue you one day. He'll start a new history with your family. Jesus will gather all of you into his family, and your lives will make a difference for heaven."

Then I cried for that little boy. He didn't deserve what came next in his life.

"Would you put the little boy someplace safe?" asked the therapist.

I pictured myself picking up the little boy and sliding him into my heart.

"I want to bring your mother in now," said the therapist.

Someone opened and shut the door. I kept my eyes closed. I knew Mom was not in the room, but I spoke to her like she was. I said things trapped in my heart since childhood, things I could not say because of Mom's fragility and my denial, things that had frozen my heart with rage.

"Mom," I screamed, "why did you beat hell into your kids? Do you have any clue how screwed up we are because of you?"

I yelled at Mom for a long time, reminding her of specific sins. Then I calmed down. I thanked her for all the good things I could think of, and then I said, "Good-bye, Mom. I love you. I'll see you soon."

Then the therapist brought Dad into the room.

"Dad," I screamed all over again. "Dad, how could you throw us away like that? Hadn't you ever heard of divorce? Leave Mom, not us. You could have been the greatest father in the world. You could have held my kids in your lap. You killed my hero."

On and on I went until I could think of no more bad things to scream at my dad. Then I calmed down and said the good things.

"I miss you, Dad," I said. "I grew up missing you because I love you. I never stopped loving you. You were the hero I wanted to be. Good, strong, smart, brave. I wish you had hung around to brag on me. I've spent my life looking for another father. I wished I could have watched you grow old. I don't know what your demons were or why you gave into them. You were hurt worse than I know. But I believe your hurts are healed now, and I can't wait to see you again."

I did not cry at Dad's funeral. I never said good-bye to him. I finally said good-bye to him in that dark room, and I gave up the tears I had saved since I was twelve years old.

The therapist brought in Poppa.

"Mr. Barley," I said, "my name is Dr. Jack Deere. I am your grandson, a fact I would not wish on anyone, you heartless, stupid bully, you child beater. Thank you for dying early. You spared all of us years of pain. My only regret is that you did not live long enough for me to pay you back. Now get out."

The therapist hesitated and then asked, "Is it all right if I bring your son Scott in?"

"Yes."

I had not written a letter to Scott.

The door opened and closed.

Before I spoke, I saw a vision of Scott. It was his first-grade picture. He was six years old. He looked like the six-year-old me in the photo on Yeager Street. He lived all of his short life never liking himself, never seeing the beauty in his life.

"Scotty, Scotty, how I miss you. You were so much like me in your recklessness. You made me laugh more than anyone. I was mad at you for so long. I'm not mad at you anymore. I was so obsessed with changing your behavior that I was oblivious to your torment. If only you were here now, I would know your pain, Scott. I'd make sure you knew in your heart that I loved you and was proud of you."

And then it was over.

It seemed like twenty minutes had passed. But the clock on the wall told me two hours had flown by.

"It's a miracle you're still alive," said one woman.

"I thought you were having a heart attack," said another. "I've never seen that much rage in anyone."

I went outside and sat on a bench behind a building. A woman wandered by, saw me sitting trance-like, and asked, "Are you okay?"

"I'm fine. Thank you," I said.

I returned to gazing at the northernmost reaches of the high Sonoran Desert. The hard, tan ground grew scattered evergreen shrubs and evergreen trees, as well as saguaro cactus. White and violet flowers bloomed randomly. The rocky ground rose up and away from me until it turned into low mountains in the distance.

The desert was still and bright at noon. The mourning doves had retreated to their roosts until late afternoon. A lone mountain wren flitted across the sky and landed in the top of a tall pine. The silent landscape was as still as my heart. Then the wren warbled a serenely sweet serenade. A warm breeze blew across my face. High above in the cloudless blue sky a red-tailed hawk drifted on the thermals. I felt light enough to float up and drift with him.

What I had been told earlier in the week must be true. Anger circulates in our bodies as negative energy until we discharge it. We can carry it for years, punishing people we love, never understanding why.

I sat on the bench for more than an hour, staring into the high desert, discovering more of its wild beauty. Until that moment, I had seen mostly barrenness when I looked at my life. Now I could see my life like the high desert. The barrenness only made the beautiful more beautiful. At last, I surrendered to the truth that I would always live in the high desert, a mixture of the bleak and the beautiful.

That photo kept coming back to my mind. I closed my eyes and stared at that six-year-old boy named Jackie, standing in his yard on Christmas Day dressed in his hero clothes. I liked that boy—such a sweet face.

It was the first time I remember liking myself.

Forty-Seven

Leesa spent three more weeks at the rehab and then left against the advice of her counselors. They told her she needed two more months in their version of a halfway house or she would drink again.

She did.

She went to two more twenty-eight-day rehabs. She loved the rehabs. But she couldn't cope with life outside them, and I settled back into my role as her personal sobriety coach.

The sounds in our house mocked my failure. Corks popped. Ice cubes tinkled in glasses. And pills rattled against plastic as they flowed into her hand.

For the first time in two years, I spoke to Scott Manley, my first Christian mentor. It was the end of August 2008. The circumstances couldn't have been worse.

Scott wanted to have his own children more than anything else in life. But Scott and Ann could not have children. So they adopted a daughter, Monica, and then a son, Guy. But Guy hated his parents. When he grew older, violence, drugs, crime, and jail became regular features of his life. At thirty-four years old, an overdose left Guy on life support.

Scott had just come home from watching the physicians disconnect his only son from the machines. I wept with him on the phone. I told him he was the greatest father I had ever known. I reminded him that I had named my second son after him.

Soon there was nothing left to say. I vowed to come to Oklahoma City so we could go fishing and drink good wine.

"I love you," I said.

"I love you too."

———

I never went fishing with Scott. In September, he went into the hospital with a mysterious flu. By the end of December, doctors diagnosed him with idiopathic pulmonary fibrosis. His lungs were scarring and thickening. He was suffocating to death. They didn't know the cause. They had no cure. Scott was claustrophobic, and I couldn't imagine a more undeserving death.

He remained so kind and cheerful that the nurses fought each other for the right to care for him as he died. Scott's secretary brought her five-year-old daughter to see Scott. The little girl sat on the bed with him. He could barely talk. Breathing was hard. Scott used some of his last breaths to tell this little one that Jesus loved her very much and always would. Scott assured the little one that Jesus would always take care of her.

Scott took his last breath less than five months after he buried his son. Life wasn't fair to him. Neither was death. He always gave more than he took.

One thousand people attended Scott's memorial service. The officiating pastor asked anyone whom Scott had impacted to stand. More than 90 percent of the room rose to their feet. The testimony to his life was silent but eloquent. The only legacy that lasts is written on the hearts you helped bring closer to heaven.

Scott did that for all of us.

———

Alcohol continued to consume Leesa's life—as did my efforts to stop her from drinking.

On September 28, 2009, I came home from a men's retreat in Colorado to find a note propped up on the kitchen counter. It was from Leesa.

"Dear Jack," it began. "I don't want to hurt you. I know this will hurt you."

Forty-Eight

When I finished reading the note, I wasn't stunned. I was stopped. My mind crashed. Fear paralyzed me.

The letter made me out to be a fallen pastor. It accused me of heartless hypocrisy, rage, financial fraud, and sexual sin. According to the letter, Leesa was a battered woman, living in terror with a religious sociopath—the man who had wrecked her world and the world of so many others. She had finally found the courage to escape.

My life was over. Lepers have more friends than fallen pastors. I would be forced into exile somewhere.

Leesa had someone hack into my computer and copy the hard drive with all of our financial records, bank account numbers, and passwords. She had someone break into the safe in my closet where I kept all of her medications. The pills and cash were gone. The filing cabinet had been emptied of financial and medical records.

The Persian rugs were gone. So was the wine from my wine cellar. Leesa's letter said she would sell these things if I cut off her credit cards.

She was starting a new life. And she would need money. She listed five things that I was not to do. At the top was that I was not to try to contact or find her. If I failed to comply with just one of her demands, she would publish the truth about me. And I would be finished.

I slept four hours that night. I waited in the darkness while the sun rose. I was on grief's time now, where "in a minute there are many days."

After the sun came up, a single verse of Scripture came to mind: "Wait for the LORD; be strong and take heart and wait for the LORD" (Psalm 27:14).

The promise that God would come into my disaster helped me endure the torment of waiting. This scary and hopeful promise forced me to make the admission I had avoided.

I really was powerless.

———

The next morning, I woke up in the dark again. I grabbed a cup of coffee and fled to my study. I didn't know if I could wait. I considered pressing my Glock pistol to my temple.

Then I saw my son Stephen's face.

Do I want to leave him like my father left me? Does ending my pain justify starting his? Do I want to cheat his kids out of a grandfather?

I banished the thought of ending my life and prayed and journaled for the rest of the morning. At noon, I called Jim, who was on a cruise in the Aegean Sea. He excused himself from dinner with Susie and their guests. I read the letter to him without edit or comment. He asked some questions about particular accusations. I told him none of the financial charges were true. Some of the other charges were.

"This is all bullshit, Jack," he said. "This is private stuff between a man and his wife."

Then he cried for me. We both knew I was headed for exile into the outer darkness.

"I love you, Jack," Jim said. "I am so glad that you're in my life."

———

On Tuesday, eight days after Leesa left, I fell asleep on the couch in front of the TV. At 10:40 p.m., my cell phone rang. "Blocked" appeared on the screen.

"Hello."

"Jack?"

"Sweetie!"

"Don't you call me sweetie. I'm not your sweetie. My name is Leesa. You call me Leesa."

My cell log recorded eight calls between 10:40 p.m. and 12:08 a.m. It was an angry recital of thirty-five years of my sins against her and others. I agreed with every accusation. But she didn't believe me. Then she hung up and called back for the next round.

At 12:08 a.m., she said, "I love you. Can I come to see you right now, for just a little while?"

"Honey, that's the best offer I've had all evening."

Five minutes later, she was at the front door. She was high, and she had been drinking. She parked at the end of the street, not in our driveway. She came into the house.

We kissed. We talked. We cried. We declared our love for each other. She left at 2 a.m., still under the influence. She declined my offer to drive her back.

Thirty minutes later, the phone rang again.

"Are you following me?"

"No, never, Sweetie."

"Then go into the bathroom and flush the toilet so I can hear it."

I put my cell phone next to the toilet and flushed.

"Thank you. I love you," she said.

"I love you too, with all my heart."

At 5 a.m., she called back.

"I'm on a freeway, out of gas," she said.

"What freeway?"

"I don't know. Eighteen-wheelers are flying by. I want to jump in front of one."

"Honey, stay in the car. Calm down. I'll find you. Can you see an exit sign?"

"Precinct Line."

"Okay. I know where you are. Do not get out of the car. I'm on my way."

Ten minutes later, I sat beside her in the Suburban. Leesa was in panic mode. All hell had broken loose. When the woman who had drawn up the blueprint for Leesa's escape discovered Leesa had come to our home to see me, Leesa said the woman "lit into" her. She berated Leesa nonstop for an hour, telling Leesa that she had ruined everything. The woman raged that now no one would believe I was an abusive husband.

Leesa said, "I'm in trouble. I broke the rules."

Her purse lay open on the console of our Suburban. I could see five bottles of pills.

I asked her to let me drive her to our home. She could sleep for a while and then figure out what she wanted to do. She said no.

The AAA driver arrived to work on Leesa's car, and I got out of the Suburban to show him my card. She locked the doors and wouldn't let me back in the car.

After the man put the gas in, she drove off into the darkness on a busy freeway, still upset and still under the influence.

Back home, I sat in my brown leather chair and wondered if I would ever see Leesa again.

Inside my head, conflicting voices abounded. One voice told me I was stupid for letting Leesa drive off drunk into the dark. Another spewed out a series of "what ifs" and trapped me in a cavalcade of contingencies. Another said all this was happening because I was a jerk.

My counselor said I should probably divorce Leesa. A friend said I should hire a lawyer and sue her friends.

In the middle of all those voices was a gentle whisper. It told me I wouldn't be judged for what my enemies do, only for what I do. Instead of focusing on getting Leesa back, I focused on that gentle whisper, trusting it to return me to sanity. The war within abated. Peace returned.

About a month later, Leesa's creditors began calling.

"This is a very important call for Leesa Deere," said the voice on the recording. "If you are not Leesa Deere, press 2."

I pressed 2.

"Are you Leesa Deere?" a real voice asked.

"Do I sound like Leesa Deere? Besides, I pressed 2. Is there something wrong with your software?"

"Do you know how to get in touch with Leesa Deere?"

"I was about to ask you the same question."

"Sir, it is very important that we get in touch with Leesa Deere."

"I feel the same way. Good luck."

"Sir, this not funny."

"I don't like smart alecks either."

"We need to reach her within seven days."

"Oh no! Are you going to cut off her credit cards? Turn her over to a collection agency?"

"Sir, we are not at liberty to talk with you about Mrs. Deere."

"Can you talk with me about Miss Campbell? That was her maiden name. She may prefer that name now."

"Sir, we are not at liberty to talk with you about Mrs. Deere."

"She told me not to use that liberty either."

I met with a counselor each week. We talked about boundaries, healthy limits on the type of interactions we will allow. Boundaries protect us, keep us from being used, and bring a sense of order to our lives. But like any good thing, they can be misused.

At the end of October, I sent Leesa a letter that told her I wanted no communication from her until she had been sober for six months. Jim questioned the wisdom of the letter.

I had told her that she had to be fixed before I would take her back. If God had treated me like that, I could never draw near to him.

Despite my growing anger, I worried that we might reach a point of no return. So I crossed the boundary I had tried to establish and sent a message to her through one of her friends.

"I want to see you," I said.

She sent word back that she wanted to see me too.

We met at the mutual friend's house the night before Thanksgiving.

I watched her get out of the car. She was phendimetrazine slim. She wore a long-sleeved white blouse and jeans. She looked beautiful and serene like the first time I saw her. She wasn't wearing her wedding ring.

She asked to hide her car in our friend's garage. She might get "caught" seeing me and be "in trouble." Her friends had been emphatic from the start: "You can never go back to Jack." They had set up an appointment with a divorce attorney, who would work pro bono, since Leesa was a battered wife. I was supposed to be served with papers next week. When she heard I wanted to see her, Leesa cancelled the appointment with the lawyer.

At the meeting, we acknowledged that we loved each other, but Leesa was not ready to come home.

A week later, she called.

"I think I'm having a nervous breakdown," she said.

The woman who had taken charge of Leesa's life would not stop berating her. Stephen was in town for the weekend. She asked that he come get her and her things.

Leesa came home. She was high and drunk. But I was grateful to have her back, even if it meant returning to our Sisyphean life.

Forty-Nine

Karen Blixen, the woman who wrote *Out of Africa*, was asked by a writer in 1957 to comment on the dismantling of her life in Africa. She said, "All sorrows can be borne if you put them into a story or tell a story about them."[1]

The people who recover from the wreckage of their trauma are the people who can write a new story for their lives where their pain betters them.

My story is about love. The boy in the picture with the Davy Crockett outfit and Jungle Jim rifle was happy because he loved and was loved. Then he learned that love would crush him, that when you loved someone, you put yourself at their mercy. You give them the power to hurt you.

The boy hated being powerless, so he built walls around himself to keep love out. But love was patient. It was kind. It kept no record of his wrongs. And it kept climbing over those walls.

When the boy became a man, love crushed him again. And again. The man saw that broken people were the hardest to love, because their wounds caused them to lash out in fear.

The man learned to diagnose the various ways in which people were broken and tried to fix them. That was safer than trying to understand and love them—just another barrier he erected.

But love is as relentless as rain that hollows out stone.

---

1. Quoted in Bent Mohn, "Talk with Isak Dinesen," *New York Times Book Review*, November 3, 1957, 49. Isak Dinesen was Blixen's pen name.

I shut the car door, and Leesa collapsed into tears. We drove home in silence from another hospital stint because of an overdose. I was angry, but I didn't show it. I was angry because she couldn't see the pain she caused those who loved her.

"The kids must hate me," she said.

"No. They love you."

"They must think I'm horrible."

"No. They're worried about you."

In the evening, I cooked dinner—blackened tuna, fresh asparagus, and salad. Then Leesa wanted to color in a child's coloring book. While I began to clean up the kitchen, she slipped into bed and cried some more. She said she was depressed and scared.

I continued in my role as doctor, pharmacist, caretaker, and parent. I couldn't remember what it was like to be Leesa's husband and friend.

An hour later, Leesa got up and went back to coloring and watching TV.

I put away the last of the dishes and sat down beside her—a fifty-seven-year-old woman searching for some self-esteem in a coloring book, trying to reclaim a stolen childhood. She tried hard to stay between the lines on the page and didn't notice my staring.

At that moment, a barrier I had built crashed down in a deluge of love that I could feel coursing through my body. I loved her as a little girl with her coloring book. I loved her as a young mother who reveled in motherhood and delighted in her three children. And I loved her as a fifty-seven-year-old woman who tottered on the abyss of insanity.

I'd never felt so much love for her. And I'd never been able to help her less.

A few months later, the young receptionist at Baylor Scott & White Medical Center in Grapevine, our favorite emergency room, studied my insurance card. She looked up and asked, "You're not Jack Deere the author, are you?"

"Guilty," I said.

"I love your books. I give them away all the time," she said.

"Thanks."

"What brings you to the emergency room at midnight?" she asked.

"The doctors are trying to revive my wife from an alcohol binge and possible pill overdose. We're not sure what she took in addition to the wine."

"Oh," she said as she looked down, "I'm sorry."

"Me too. Thanks."

I filled out the admission forms and went back into the emergency room. Leesa had regained a woozy consciousness. The slender, gray-haired doctor held a cup full of thick gray liquid. He explained that it was a charcoal cocktail meant to neutralize any sleeping pills she might have taken.

"If you don't swallow every bit of this, we will pump your stomach. And that experience will not be nearly as pleasant as drinking the charcoal."

Without a word, she threw her head back and gulped down the nasty concoction as though it were a small bottle of Pinot Grigio.

That night, I prayed in her room until she fell asleep because I would rather be terrified beside Leesa's ICU bed than be happy in a mansion with someone else.

When I wasn't rescuing Leesa from her binges or playing golf with friends, I stood on a stage and told people that God loves us, even though we are pretty screwed up. I told them that sometimes, at my worst moments, God overpowers me with his affection.

Almost nothing in my life has worked out like I thought it

should. I thought as I grew older, I would grow more deserving of God's love, not less.

While Leesa bounced from binge to binge, I lived from failure to failure.

A young executive from Cincinnati visited my church.

"I love your books," she said. "I listen to your sermons online all the time."

I invited her to come to lunch with a few of my friends after the service.

"That would be wonderful," she said. Then she hesitated for a second and said, "I thought there would be thousands of people here."

"Me too," I said.

I sent a draft of a book I had worked on for five years to a successful author friend. She returned it with handwritten criticisms. The space between her criticisms increased. Then they stopped altogether. She was too polite to tell me my book was not salvageable.

I couldn't write. I couldn't build a church. I couldn't get my wife sober.

So every morning, I sat in my brown leather overstuffed chair in the center of my study, and for the first time in my life, I prayed more than I studied. I asked God to search my heart and expose the offensive things. I asked him to grant me grace to gaze on his beauty.

I saw that I too was a broken person who lashed out in fear.

Gabor Maté wrote, "People jeopardize their lives for the sake of making the moment livable."[2]

---

2. Gabor Maté, *In the Realm of Hungry Ghosts: Close Encounters with Addiction* (Berkeley, CA: North Atlantic, 2008), 29.

Somewhere I heard that telling a person who has been trapped in an addiction for years to stop is like filling up a person with laxatives and then telling them not to poop.

I had tried to save Leesa by laying down laws, taking away things, and threatening her. When my affection dried up, she turned to the warmth of dopamine hugs and serotonin kisses given to her by alcohol and opioids.

When I told people what I had endured, they pitied me. But she was the true sufferer. She grew up abused, abandoned, and shamed. The childhood stress helped hardwire her for addiction.

But she couldn't remember a time when she did not love God.

She did not drink when we married. I brought wine into our home.

For thousands of days, I prayed for Leesa's sobriety. I prayed for my church to grow. I prayed to be able to write. God said no. Again and again. Then the lecturer ran out of lectures. I was powerless not only over alcohol but over life as well. My efforts to sober up Leesa made her suffering worse.

Yet she was still standing—not tall, not straight, but standing. Anyone else would have fallen long ago.

Each day, a drinking alcoholic who no longer saw beauty in herself became more beautiful to me.

In mid-November 2011, I sat on the couch with the *Wall Street Journal*. Our home had been tranquil for almost three weeks, but Leesa had not come out of the bedroom that morning. If we stayed true to our routine, another binge loomed.

Leesa knew she wasn't safe, and she agreed with the one restriction I put on her: that she couldn't drive. She didn't want to be responsible for harming another family.

At eleven o'clock she still hadn't come out of the bedroom. I had accepted the fact that, apart from divine intervention, one day she wouldn't come out of the bedroom. *Accepted* meant I had renounced coercion, manipulation, and lies as a means of changing her. *Accepted* meant I prayed for Leesa and enjoyed her today—while I could.

Half an hour later, Leesa still hadn't emerged from the bedroom. I thought maybe I should check on her. She had gone to bed sober last night, but that didn't mean she would wake up sober.

I didn't want to open our bedroom door. Every time I put my right hand on the doorknob, fear pricks my heart. It has been nine years and eleven months since the morning I opened the door to Scott's bedroom. The thought of opening our bedroom door releases an album of pictures in my brain.

I put the newspaper down. I swallowed. I sighed. I stood.

Leesa walked in wearing a blue blouse and jeans. She looked serious. She had a pill bottle in her right hand.

"Jack, I want to stop drinking now. I want you to give me Antabuse every morning," she said, and then she handed me a bottle of Antabuse.

Antabuse (disulfiram) blocks the liver's ability to metabolize alcohol. So the person who drinks alcohol after taking Antabuse skips the euphoria stage and goes straight to the hangover, but it's not a normal hangover. It's a hangover times ten to the tenth power. A couple of years ago, Leesa drank while she was on Antabuse. Her head exploded. She thought she was having a stroke. She threw up until the dry heaves racked her abdomen, and she felt her stomach crawling up her esophagus. She never drank on Antabuse again. But after a few weeks of not drinking, she refused to take Antabuse.

That morning, she wanted to try Antabuse again. Hope rose in me. The Antabuse was her idea. I hadn't suggested it. I no longer suggested anything.

Each morning after that, I ground up the Antabuse tablet and stirred the powder into half a glass of water, and Leesa gulped it down. I ground up the tablet and dissolved it in water so Leesa couldn't hide the tablet under her tongue and spit it out after I left the room. After she downed her morning sobriety drink, she drank coffee and hung out with me for about thirty minutes, so she had no opportunity to secretly throw up the medicine.

On the rare mornings when I forgot her medicine, she would bring it to me.

After a while, Leesa became interested in things. She started different art projects. She hung out with friends. Our social life was resurrected. Leesa brought the children of our young friends over to color, draw, paint, or make cards for hours at a time. Some evenings, I heard Leesa and her friends laughing upstairs in Leesa's art room.

Laughter.

I didn't realize how much I missed Leesa's laughter. Her laughter is pure. She is too honest for courtesy laughter. Some weekends, she and her friend Debby and one or two others checked into a hotel in the middle of our outdoor mall for a weekend girls' slumber party.

Weeks without a drink turned into months, and then a year.

Fifty

On April 9, 2011, I performed the wedding ceremony for Stephen and his bride, Lindsay. A year later, Rachel Marie Deere entered my world. She had brown hair, fair skin, and blue eyes. I wanted my first grandchild to be a son. I was so stupid. I had no idea of the perfect little beauty God had waited to give me. Give *me*? I sound like a father now. I'm only a grandfather. But I don't feel like a grandfather. How is a grandfather supposed to feel? I didn't know it would feel this good.

Yes, I'd had three babies of my own. I marveled at them. I loved them. But I had them too soon. I was too preoccupied with building my kingdom. I didn't enjoy them as much as I could have. I have more time than I've ever had, but I'm not retired. I'm focused on enjoying the ones I love and the One I love. And that counts for more than what I'm building.

On Memorial Day 2012, I listened to my son read Rachel a bedtime story. This was their nightly routine. She was two months old during this bedtime story. Lindsay held Rachel and leaned into Stephen. I sat beside the family of three on their worn, velvety, chocolate brown couch. Leesa stretched out on the floor of their loft in downtown St. Louis. Stephen opened the book so Rachel could see the pictures. He read the words using different accents. He had to fight off his own laughter. Lindsay laughed too. Rachel giggled and touched the pictures.

I looked at Leesa stretched out on the floor, basking in the love of her son for his wife and baby girl. At last, her world was sober, right, and happy. I stared at Leesa, and I saw another baby girl who never enjoyed a scene like this, a baby girl to whom a single book was never read, who was left alone with caretakers, who was used as a sexual object by her father, and who went undefended by her mother, who became jealous of her.

"I hate you," the little girl's mother once said to her. "You make me want to kill myself."

Then I remembered that little girl at twenty-two as she held her infant son Stephen, sang to him, and prayed over him. She was enraptured with love for her baby boy, confident that at last she walked in the purposes for which she had been created, and thankful to the God who created her, thankful to God who made her what she always and only ever wanted to be—a wife and a mother. I saw that young mother read stories to her infant son— stories that were never read to her—not out of obligation, but because it made her happy to read to her baby boy.

I recalled Stephen pulling her long brown hair and rubbing the pages of the books. Stephen learned to talk a little, and I saw Leesa read to him all the Beatrix Potter books. A little later, when he could follow bigger stories, Leesa read *Charlotte's Web* to him. It was the first time for both of them, and they cried together over Charlotte's death at the end.

While I built my kingdom, Leesa built a home in Stephen's heart for God.

Now Rachel will grow up loved, delighted in, feeling beautiful and smart, with her dignity and defenses intact.

As I watched the scene unfold, I was filled with awe at my wife. She could have turned bitter. Instead, she had chosen love.

The curse under which she was born had been shattered.

———

In *East of Eden*, John Steinbeck wrote that we all have one story, and it is the same story: the contest of good and evil within us.[1] Any honest person knows that they are losing this contest.

As a child, I could lie to others, but hadn't yet developed the sophistication to lie to myself. I knew my bad deeds would always push down the scale. So I chose to enjoy my darkness rather than feel guilty about it.

Then I discovered that Christ had already borne the weight of my sin, and that once I accepted his gift, he would never leave. Yet Saint Peter's scales lingered. In church I was told that as a Christian, my good deeds eventually would outweigh the bad. Then I preached versions of the same message.

But the evidence always contradicted the promise. My life stayed messy. I never stopped needing God's mercy.

I once took the biggest piece of pie without a twinge of guilt. After I became a Christian, I never did that again. I manipulated people into giving me the biggest piece of pie, and I thought myself clever. I didn't become a better Christian—only a Christian more sophisticated in his evil.

I am not the first to make this confession. It's in the biographies of many great believers in both Scripture and later history. The purest people claim to be riddled with impurity. The humblest saints claim to be ruled by monstrous pride. At the end of his life, the apostle Paul claimed that he was the chief of sinners (1 Timothy 1:15). He didn't write, "I *was* the chief of sinners," but "I *am* the chief of sinners."

The closer Paul drew to the Light of the world, the more evil he saw in his life.

I am no great believer. I wish I could make Paul's confession. Maybe one day I will. But I can confess with Paul, "In my flesh dwelleth no good thing" (Romans 7:18 KJV). I am more aware of

---

1. John Steinbeck, *East of Eden* (New York: Penguin, 2016), 413.

the enormity of evil in me than I've ever been. This is one way I can tell that the light within me is expanding.

One truly good person was born into this world. This is the truth. If it were the only truth, then Albert Camus would have been right: suicide is a legitimate consideration. But there is another great truth.

"I no longer call you servants . . . Instead, I have called you friends" (John 15:15), Jesus told his disciples on the eve of his crucifixion.

He said this over a meal.

The only truly good and holy person wants to be our friend despite our messiness and all our failed attempts to clean ourselves up.

The harmony of these two truths is the seed from which obedience flourishes.

My first memory is of Dad carrying me through the basement of a department store. His arms never rested to put me down. By the cash register lay a pocket knife. It looked just like the one he carried.

I begged him for it and cried when he handed me the rubber imitation.

Dad could have told me that a two-year-old lacks the fine motor skills to carry a knife and that giving me a blade would have only produced blood. But I would not have understood.

For years, I have besieged heaven with thousands of prayers that seemed to go unanswered. Still, I return to that brown leather chair. It is old and worn like me, but I lean back and let it hold me. As I close my eyes, I can sometimes sense the Spirit of God hovering.

When I lusted after material wealth, he turned my gaze toward eternity. When I sought large crowds, he brought me humility. When I tried to change my wife, he taught me how to love and understand her.

What I really needed all along, more than anything, was to see myself through his eyes.

————————

Now I have more days like this one.

It is Saturday, June 11, 2012. The flicker of dawn creeps into my study. I want to see God's beauty. But I'm also trying to find something to say. My Sunday stage waits for me. As usual, my motives are mixed.

I open my Bible to Psalm 27:4.

> One thing I ask from the LORD,
>   this only do I seek:
> that I may dwell in the house of the LORD
>   all the days of my life,
> to gaze on the beauty of the LORD
>   and to seek him in his temple.

These six lines are the essence of all of King David's psalms.

So on this morning, I tell God I want to gaze on his beauty. But I'm not sure how to go about it. I'm not sure I know how to define his beauty.

Artists and poets, theologians and philosophers, have argued over beauty for thousands of years. Aquinas's definition of beauty is one of the most famous: beauty is what gives us pleasure when seen. But that definition is too tame for me. I survey some of Aquinas's modern disciples and cobble together this definition: beauty is a mysterious harmony that dazzles us.

It is not one feature of the *Mona Lisa* that makes her beautiful; it is the harmony of all her features. Change one of the features, and the magic diminishes.

My first sunset over the Pacific Ocean dazzled me. My first

hearing of Beethoven's Ninth Symphony dazzled me. Leesa dazzled me when she climbed out of that yellow Pontiac coupe.

But after a couple of hours, I am not dazzled. I have searched in all the usual places: Bibles, lexicons, concordances, and commentaries. But this morning, God has not hidden his beauty in books.

I walk out of my study and lie down on the guest bed. I vow to stay prostrate until God dazzles me. Maybe my persistence will impress him. For more than an hour, I rummage through my history with God. I recall acts of his mercy, goodness, and forgiveness, but I am left undazzled.

My smartphone pings with an email. I pull the phone out of my pocket. There is a video. I forget my vow. I walk back to my computer in my study and sit down in my big brown leather chair. The video is eighteen seconds long. I watch it over and over. Every time I push *Play*, I think: *This is the last time I will watch the video. I need to get back to God.* Then I push *Play* again.

On the screen, Rachel lies on her back and giggles. Lindsay and Lindsay's mother, Melanie, are both off camera, saying, "Say gou, Rachel. Say gou."

Rachel wiggles about and lifts her hands high in the air. She smiles and says, "Gou," her first syllable at two months old.

It is one moment among millions that will make up her existence, and yet I want to remain in this moment for as long as possible.

A pang of sadness surfaces. She is growing up fast, and I will miss so much of her life if we stay in separate cities. I want to jump on a plane.

I keep watching and watching. I laugh at myself. In my laughter is the gentle whisper.

This is how I feel about you, it says.

I shake. I reach for the keyboard. Before I touch the keys, my chest heaves with joy. He has taken an angry ten-year-old boy

surrounded by presents on Christmas morning and turned him into
an old man awash in gratitude for a child's gibberish.

When at last I can speak, I say, "Thank you. Thank you.
Thank you."

Acknowledgments

There is a minimal amount of coarse language in my book. None of it is gratuitous. I am grateful that Zondervan felt, as I do, that to tell my story any other way would have been to diminish its authenticity and power.

Only three names have been changed in this story: Charlotte, Alex, and Mary.

John Sloan, Zondervan's specialist in editing memoirs, was helpful in showing me the architecture of a memoir and keeping my story on track. Ryan Pazdur, the editor who supervised the work from beginning to end, has been a great believer in my story and extraordinarily patient with many last-minute changes. Dirk Buursma brought more than thirty years of experience in copy editing to polish the final version of my memoir. I am grateful to Stan Gundry, senior vice president at Zondervan, who pursued me over the years, even though I hadn't published anything in more than a decade.

My friends Christopher Ave and Winston Calvert read every line of the book, made many valuable suggestions, and corrected faults that I could not see.

I will always be grateful for the love of our close friends who took care of our family when we could not take care of ourselves. Of those wonderful people, John and Nancy Snyder stand out. There has not been any time limit or geographical limit to their love for us. Nancy is with the Lord now. Mark and Nancy Duarte gave Scott a home when we couldn't. We are even closer today. We count each other as family. Mark and Nancy suffered through this manuscript in its verbose earlier stages. I had written ten pages on what it was like to be in an Old Testament doctoral program. Nancy wrote in the margin of those pages, "Why do I care about this?" Those ten egotistical, self-indulgent pages have been condensed into two sentences that are still not entirely free of egotism.

One of the pains in writing this book is that some of my best sentences lie on the cutting floor because the story took a turn that wouldn't permit them. One of the best friends I have ever had lies on the cutting floor as well. Dudley Hall and I have traveled around the world together, speaking at conferences and churches. We have hunted all over our country together. After we lost Scott, we left Montana and moved into a house in Fort Worth five minutes from Dudley. For months, he called and came by every day, looking for ways to help us.

My son Stephen Deere is an award-winning journalist. He has been my best critic and editor. He has shown me features of my story that I could never have seen on my own. More than anyone else, he has made this a better book than I could ever have written by myself.

Then there is Leesa, who has been my partner for most of my story. She has endured more trauma than anyone I know, and yet she still loves God and people. Instead of hiding the abuse of her childhood and her adult struggle with alcoholism, she has stood on a stage and told her story to other women, who have wept and been freed from the prison of their secrets. She has read every unflattering line I have written about her in this book with the hope that her story will help others find the freedom that she lives in now. Next to God she is the hero of my story.

For years, I refused to speak publicly about my son's death. I did not want to be like a preacher in a John Updike novel who "forges God's name on every sentence he speaks." In those years,

I was also learning that when the worst day of your life comes, it is only the beginning of bad. Suddenly, it seemed like everybody had a better story than mine. Then my story got worse. God took away just about everything I used to fuel my self-esteem until there was nothing left except his love. And for the first time, I felt his love apart from anything I could offer him. And then I no longer needed a better story.